National Aeronautics and Space Administration

I0178627

Nose Up

High Angle-of-Attack and Thrust Vectoring Research at NASA Dryden 1979-2001

Lane E. Wallace

Edited by
Christian Gelzer

National Aeronautics and Space Administration
NASA History Office
Washington, D.C.
2005

ll

Library of Congress Cataloging-in-Publication Data

Wallace, Lane E., 1961-
  Nose up : high angle-of-attack and thrust vectoring research at NASA Dryden, 1979-2001 / Lane E.
Wallace ; edited by Christian Gelzer.
      p. cm.
  Includes bibliographical references.
  1. NASA Dryden Flight Research Center--Research--History. 2. Airplanes--Motors--Thrust--
Research--United States--History. 3. Angle of attack (Aerodynamics)--Research--United States--
History. I. Title.
  TL521.312.W43 2004
  623.74'64--dc22

Contents

Forward

NASA's Dryden Flight Research Center has been the focal point for an extraordinary number of important flight programs. It was here in the Mojave Desert that the speed of sound was first surpassed in flight; where aircraft first flew to space and reentered the atmosphere; where humans learned how to land on the moon; where digital fly-by-wire controls were perfected; and solar-powered airplanes proved their mettle. And it was here, at the crossroads of flight research, that three different programs explored high-alpha flight, that is, flight at high angles of attack (AoA). From these programs came fundamental knowledge of a largely unexplored region of flight, as well as validation of new means of controlling aircraft in the post-stall regime. As in the past, Dryden researchers helped redefine flight. Lane Wallace's Nose Up: High Angle-of-Attack and Thrust Vectoring Research at NASA Dryden, 1979-2001, represents the first historical assessment of these programs.

High angles of attack usually precede a stall, which most pilots try to avoid. While some aircraft exhibit fairly benign manners at high alpha and in a stall, not all do. Little attention was paid to this part of the flight envelope largely because few saw any reason to intentionally risk an aircraft in this regime. It was best avoided, and at worst something to learn how to recover from. But researchers at NASA, several aerospace companies, and several government agencies were curious to know about aspects of high-alpha flight. Out of this curiosity came three distinct flight research programs.

The F-18 HARV (High Alpha Research Vehicle) was a joint project between two NASA centers, Langley and Dryden, involving a heavily modified McDonnell Douglas F-18. The X-31, an entirely original aircraft and the first international X-plane program, was initially headed for flight testing at the Navy's Patuxent River facility in Maryland, but the program came to Dryden instead, barely fifty miles up the road from the Lockheed plant in Palmdale where the experimental planes were built. The McDonnell Douglas F-15 ACTIVE (Advanced Controls Technology for Integrated Vehicles) came to Dryden after a tour with the Air Force at Edwards Air Force Base, a mile down the ramp, and it, too, was extensively modified.

Each of the programs focused on thrust vectoring as the key to high-alpha maneuvering. This involves directing engine exhaust during flight to enhance the control of the airplane. Along the way the participants developed and demonstrated new technologies, not least of which was the means itself of vectoring jet engine thrust. Two of the aircraft did this with vanes that deflected the exhaust; the third experimented with exhaust nozzles that swiveled.

The three programs also highlighted the organizational flexibilities at Dryden. Partnering with other NASA centers is not new; it has long been the practice of capitalizing on the strengths of various centers for a common goal, and Dryden's own record of collaborating with industry goes back to its very first days beside Rogers Dry Lake in the Mojave Desert. The HARV and F-15 ACTIVE programs involved NASA and industry members, as well as branches of the U.S. military. But the X-31 program in particular illustrated several changes in the way NASA and its industry partners do business. As an international experimental aircraft program it involved elements of the U.S. government (NASA, DARPA, the U.S. Navy), the American aerospace firm Lockheed Aircraft, the German aerospace firm Messerschmitt-Bölkow-Blohm, and a branch of the German Ministry of Defense. The X-31 program united a host of differing interests and methods and proved a genuine success. In many respects the program peaked during a captivating display of the aircraft's performance at the Paris Air Show in 1995, where an international audience witnessed for the first time just what thrust vectoring could do.

This monograph maps the histories of each program and their contributions to aviation. Between the pages, however, is the story of the nation's premier flight research center and its partnerships with industry. As it has in the past, Dryden serves the aviation community and a nation as it advances the science of flight.

Christian Gelzer

Acknowledgments

I am especially grateful to Dr. John D. Hunley, then Chief Historian at Dryden Flight Research Center, under whose auspices this project began. I am also grateful to the many people who sat for interviews for this project and answered my follow-up questions. I am also indebted to those who supplied me notes, viewgraphs, correspondence, reports, and other printed material from their personal files.
Lane Wallace

Thanks also extend to a number of people at Dryden who helped in the layout and production of this monograph, among them: Mike Gorn, then Chief Historian, who ushered this project through; Carla Thomas of the Photo Lab, who scanned the images; Ted Huetter for the wonderful layout; and Sarah Merlin of the X-Press, for copy editing.
Christian Gelzer

Contributors

Associate Editor: Sarah Merlin

Book Design and Layout: Ted Huetter

Photography: Jim Ross, Carla Thomas, Tom Tschida

Illustrations: Dave Faust

Introduction

WHY NOSE UP?

At 2:20 in the afternoon of June 10, 1995, Rockwell test pilot Fred Knox lifted off from Le Bourget airport to begin the first flight demonstration of the Rockwell/MBB X-31A research aircraft at the Paris Air Show. With a delta wing/canard design, a General Electric 404 turbine engine, and aft-end paddles that could direct its engine exhaust up, down, and sideways, the X-31A bore little resemblance to any airplane performing that year or any years before.

By turning, or vectoring, the thrust from the X-31's engine exhaust nozzle, the research plane was able to accomplish astonishing feats of maneuverability while flying at extremely low speeds and dramatically high angles of attack that would have sent conventional jet fighters out of control.[1] The technology that made the X-31's accomplishments possible needed refinement, and there was still much to be learned about thrust-vectoring. But for those who witnessed it, the X-31's Paris flights irrevocably changed perceptions of an airplane's capabilities, at least in the world outside the research labs of the National Aeronautics and Space Administration (NASA) and its military and industry partners. After the impressive, public, low-level demonstration of the X-31's abilities, few doubted whether thrust-vectoring was possible. What remained were questions about the practical issues of need, application, and the costs versus the benefits of this new technological capability.

Vectoring an aircraft's thrust enables two things of importance to fighter aircraft. The first is increased maneuverability, since vectoring the jet's exhaust allows the aircraft to turn more sharply and rapidly that a conventional fighter. The second is flight at very steep angles of attack, angles that cause conventional aircraft to stall and depart controlled flight. Both abilities are an advantage for aircraft engaged in combat, hence the concept's appeal in military circles.

The applications of thrust-vectoring will depend on the needs and priorities of the military or potential commercial customers. But much of the information needed to analyze the potential of thrust-vectoring and flight maneuvers at unusual attitudes now exists. This knowledge derives from three research projects, the X-31, the High Alpha Research Vehicle (HARV), and the Advanced Controls Technology for Integrated Vehicles (ACTIVE), all of which were conducted in cooperation with NASA.

The X-31 program, which lasted from 1986 to 1995, was an international research effort focusing on investigating the tactical potential of a highly maneuverable fighter aircraft with thrust-vectoring capability. During that same period, NASA's High Alpha Technology Program (HATP) used a highly modified F-18 with thrust-vectoring capability to investigate and define the complex aerodynamic phenomena that occur at the high angles of attack and unusual attitudes made possible by the use of thrust-vectoring. As the F-18 and X-31 programs wound down, a third NASA research project began investigating the dynamics of thrust-vectoring across a much broader spectrum of a fighter's flight envelope, including supersonic flight. This program, called the Advanced Controls Technology for Integrated Vehicles (ACTIVE), employed a highly modified F-15 fighter equipped with a thrust-vectoring nozzle that more closely resembled what might be used in a production design. In addition to generating data about the forces and dynamics involved in vectoring a jet engine's thrust, the F-15 ACTIVE program evaluated the strengths and weaknesses of thrust-vectoring nozzle design.

The partnership of NASA and various branches of the US military, as well as the West German Ministry of Defense, yielded both flight data and pilot experience in area of high-alpha flight, a region unexplored at that time. This is the story of those three programs, and the three aircraft at the heart of these thrust-vectoring experiments.

---

[1] Angle of attack, or "alpha," is an aeronautical term which describes the angle of aircraft's wing relative to its flight path. Put another way, it is the angle at which the air from the aircraft's flight path (or velocity vector) hits the wing. An aircraft in stable, level flight would have an angle-of-attack close to zero. If an aircraft was moving forward at a stable altitude but had its nose pointed up 20-degrees, the angle-of-attack of the wing would be close to 20 degrees. A 20-degree angle-of-attack could also be achieved, however, if the aircraft was in a horizontal configuration but was descending at a 20-degree angle. In either case, the air from the aircraft's flight path would be hitting the wing at a 20-degree angle. Angle of attack is always relative to the path of the aircraft through the air: it does not matter if the aircraft is climbing, descending or maintaining level flight.

Chapter One
Origins and Evolution

The concept of using thrust as a control device is not a new one. Robert Goddard invented two types of thrust-vectoring controls on sounding rockets that he tested in the 1930s, and the Germans incorporated thrust-vectoring controls in the V-2 missiles used to attack other European countries during World War II.[1] Even the use of thrust-vectoring as a control device for aircraft is not new. The Hawker Harrier (originally called the Kestrel), which first flew in 1960 and went into service in 1969, used a system of turning louvers in the fuselage underneath the wings that could vector the jet's thrust downward, enabling it to take off and land vertically.[2] But the idea of thrust-vectoring to enhance aircraft maneuverability began to generate interest among researchers and the military in large part because of aircraft losses sustained during and after the Vietnam War.[3]

In the late 1950s and 1960s, the design of most U.S. fighter aircraft pivoted on the concept of speed. It was a philosophy that many in the military and aircraft industry distilled simply as "speed is life." By then fighters were seen as high-speed missile platforms that would not necessarily even need guns because their anticipated combat would consist of standoff missile launches far away from actual adversaries. Their survivability would hinge on speed, which would allow them to get into a target area, launch their missiles, and get out quickly.

The rules of engagement in Vietnam, however, required closer visual identification of targets, and fighter pilots in F-105s and F-4s soon found themselves in close-in engagements with much more agile and maneuverable Soviet-made MiGs. Put into situations where they were required to maneuver sharply, the designed-for-speed American fighters did not fare well. Over 100 F-4 Phantom jets were lost in the Vietnam War era in loss-of-control accidents that occurred after their pilots got into high-angle-of-attack, or high "alpha" situations.[4]

There were two issues facing pilots and designers of the period. First was a clear need to improve the maneuvering ability of U.S. fighters. Second was how to achieve that increased maneuverability without losing aircraft to stall-spin accidents. The initial efforts to address both issues came through pilot training, since technological changes took longer to develop. Air combat maneuvering training such as that taught at the Navy's "Top Gun" school became a bigger priority. At the same time, operational procedures for many fighters were modified, and pilots were instructed to make careful, precise control inputs at high angles of attack in order to limit the use of high-alpha maneuvers.[5]

There was also a push during the 1970s to develop technology that would increase aircraft maneuverability and prevent aircraft losses from stall-spin accidents. A national stall-spin accident conference held in Dayton, Ohio, in 1971 emphasized the military's increasing concern over aircraft losses.[6] The Navy's F-14 Tomcat fighter, flown for the first time on 21 December 1970, was too far along in the design cycle for radical changes to be incorporated into its design. But proposals for the next generation of fighters stressed requirements for better maneuverability and better high-alpha capabilities.[7]

At the same time, technological advancements in other areas were making these desired improvements more achievable. On 25 May 1972, the NASA Flight

[1] George Sutton, email document to author regarding early use of thrust-vectoring control in rocket design, 22 January 2002.

[2] Michael J.H. Taylor, ed., *Jane's Encyclopedia of Aviation* (New York: Portland House, 1989), 114-115; Joseph R. Chambers, *Partners in Freedom* (Washington, D.C.: National Aeronautics and Space Administration, NASA Monographs in Aerospace History Number 19, 2000), 11-18.

[3] Chambers, *Partners in Freedom*, 43-44, 215; Joseph R. Chambers. Interviewed by Lane E. Wallace, 15 August 2001, transcript, DFRC Historical Reference Collection, (all interviews are tape recordings with transcriptions, and reside in the Dryden Flight Research Historical Reference Collection); Col. Michael Francis, USAF (Ret.), interviewed by author, Burlingame, CA, 14 February 2002.

[4] Viewgraph, NASA Dryden Flight Research Center Historical Reference Collection, (hereafter DFRC Historical Reference Collection) undated; Chambers, *Partners in Freedom*, 32; "High Alpha Technology Program (HATP) Plan," 19 March 1990, DFRC Historical Reference Collection; Chambers, interviewed by author, 15 August 2001; Dan Murri, interviewed by author, 14 August 2001.

[5] Albion Bowers, "F-18 High Alpha Research Vehicle Overview," 1995, draft, DFRC Historical Reference Collection.

Research Center (now the Dryden Flight Research Center) at Edwards Air Force Base, California, flew the first digital fly-by-wire aircraft, a modified F-8.[8] Development of fly-by-wire technology, which allowed more precise, computer-controlled flight control inputs, gave both the Air Force's F-16 Falcon and the Navy's F-18 Hornet much better handling characteristics than those of previous fighter designs. But the F-16 still had to use alpha limiters to keep pilots from getting the airplane into flight attitudes from which it would depart controlled flight. The controllability and agility of even the newer F-15 and F-18 fighters still deteriorated at high angles of attack because of the relative ineffectiveness of their aerodynamic controls in those conditions, and the loss-of-control accidents continued. From 1977 to 1987, the U.S. military lost no fewer than 177 aircraft to stall-spin accidents. Clearly, the goal of "safe, carefree maneuvering" had not yet been achieved.[9]

Fly-by-wire technology, however, was not the only new development being investigated by researchers in the search for better and safer maneuverability for fighter aircraft. Dryden used an F-111 research aircraft to test the first digital electronic engine control system in 1976.[10] Digital engine control was a critical step in developing any sophisticated thrust-vectoring control system because it made possible a thrust-vectoring system that was transparent to the pilot. With an integrated digital flight and engine control system, a computer would sense the pilot's control inputs and then both determine and command an optimal combination of responses from both the flight control surfaces and the engine or engines in order to make the aircraft respond appropriately.

Researchers also were beginning to investigate the concept and possibilities of vectoring, or turning, an aircraft's exhaust as a means of improving various aspects of aircraft performance. As early as the mid-1960s, researchers in the Propulsion Aerodynamics Branch at the NASA Langley Research Center in Hampton, Virginia, began examining the possibility of adding two-dimensional thrust-vectoring nozzles (nozzles able to vector the jet's exhaust up or down in pitch, but not side to side in yaw) to the F-111 "Aardvark's" engines in order to reduce the aircraft's aft-end drag.[11]

In the early 1970s, the Navy began examining two-dimensional thrust-vectoring nozzles as a way of improving the vertical, or short takeoff and landing, capabilities of high-performance aircraft. A General Electric design called the Augmented Deflector Exhaust Nozzle (ADEN) was selected as a particularly promising concept, and following a joint NASA and Department of Defense two-dimensional nozzle workshop in 1975, three potential flight research projects for the concept were considered employing three different aircraft: an F-15, an F-16, and an F-18. Full-scale tests of an ADEN nozzle were conducted in a 1976 altitude test cell at NASA Lewis Research Center, Cleveland, Ohio (now Glenn Research Center), and scale model research of an F-18 modified with the ADEN nozzles also was conducted in Langley's 16-Foot Transonic Wind Tunnel.[12]

But funding to take any of those two-dimensional tests any further did not materialize, although a two-dimensional thrust-vectoring and reversing nozzle was flight tested on a highly modified F-15 Short Take Off and Landing/Maneuver Technology Demonstrator (S/MTD) at Edwards Air Force Base in the 1980s. The primary goal of the S/MTD program was to investigate technologies that would enable fighters to be operated successfully from bomb-damaged

---

[6] The conference, sponsored by the Air Force Flight Dynamics Laboratory and the Aeronautical Systems Division and officially called the "Stall/Post-Stall/Spin Symposium," took place at Wright-Patterson Air Force Base (OH) on 15-17 December 1971. The impetus for the conference, according to Joseph Chambers, was a memo from Grant Hansen, USAF Assistant Secretary of R&D, to the Air Force research organizations expressing deep concern over the USAF losses to stall/spin accidents. The USAF had lost 147 aircraft (of all categories) to stall/spin/out of control factors in the five-year period from 1966-1970. Chambers, interviewed by author, 15 August 2001.

[7] Chambers, interviewed by author, 15 August 2001; Chambers, *Partners in Freedom*, 32-36.

[8] James E. Tomayko, *Computers Take Flight: A History of NASA's Pioneering Digital Fly-by-Wire Project* (Washington, D.C.: National Aeronautics and Space Administration, NASA SP-2000-4224, 2000), vii-x.

[9] "High Alpha Technology Program (HATP) Plan," 19 March 1990; Joseph R. Chambers, interviewed by author, 15 August 2001.

[10] Frank W. Burcham, Jr., et. al., "Propulsion Flight Research at NASA Dryden from 1967 to 1997," NASA TP-1998-206554, July 1998, 2.

[11] Chambers, interviewed by author, 15 August 2001; Chambers, *Partners in Freedom*, 68-71.

or very short runways. A secondary objective was to evaluate potential technologies for the upcoming Advanced Tactical Fighter (ATF) program. Planning for the F-15 S/MTD program began in 1984, and the first flight took place on 10 May 1989. Results of the F-15 S/MTD program showed that two-dimensional thrust-vectoring and thrust-reversing nozzles could, among other things, significantly improve takeoff and landing performance. The various research efforts with two-dimensional thrust-vectoring nozzles also indicated that use of the technology could improve an aircraft's performance in numerous other areas. Some of these improvements included reducing an aircraft's trim drag and enhancing its maneuverability and takeoff/landing performance, as well as potential reductions to an aircraft's infrared signature. As a result, two-dimensional thrust-vectoring nozzles were incorporated into Lockheed-Martin's Advanced Tactical Fighter, the F-22 Raptor. The Raptor prototype, the YF-22, with two-dimensional thrust-vectoring nozzles on its Pratt & Whitney F119-PW-100 engines, flew for the first time on 29 September 1990.[13]

Meanwhile, researchers in the late 1970s and 1980s were beginning to evaluate the possibilities of using three-dimensional thrust-vectoring (in pitch and yaw) to enhance the maneuverability and controllability of high-performance aircraft, especially at high angles of attack. Engineers in Langley's Flight Dynamics Branch had done simulations and free-flying model tests to determine what effect three-dimensional thrust-vectoring nozzles would have on various high-performance aircraft. An ADEN nozzle modified with side-door capability to allow vectoring in yaw as well as pitch, for example, was put on an X-29 model and tested in Langley's full-scale wind tunnel in 1984. The X-29 wind-tunnel tests indicated that a three-dimensional thrust-vectoring nozzle could effectively enhance the X-29's controllability at extremely high angles of attack.

Langley engineers also tried three-dimensional thrust-vectoring nozzles on other free-flying models, including an F-16 and F-15, testing them in Langley's 30- by 60-foot wind tunnel. The results were impressive. Researchers found that with multi-axis thrust-vectoring, they could fly an F-16 down to zero air speed, at angles of attack approaching 90 degrees.[14]

Military researchers also were beginning to show a greater interest in multi-axis thrust-vectoring. The Navy's F-14 Tomcat fighter had been plagued by a high accident rate due to loss of control/spin accidents. Various potential solutions had been developed, including installation of an Aileron Rudder Interconnect (ARI), but the problem persisted. In the early 1980s, the Navy and NASA conducted a joint piloted simulation study in Langley's differential maneuvering simulator to examine potential benefits of multi-axis thrust-vectoring for improving control of the F-14, especially at high angles of attack. Several of the F-14 losses resulted from asymmetric thrust situations, which occurred when the fighter lost one of its two engines, and Dave Lacey, a researcher at the Navy's David Taylor Model Basin, in Bethesda, Maryland, thought that thrust-vectoring might help maintain control during an engine-out scenario. The results of the piloted-simulation study were encouraging enough that Lacey began to look for cost-effective ways to flight test such a thrust-vectoring concept.

Lacey began experimenting with potential thrust-vectoring methods on a small scale, using bent spoons behind a small engine model to see if paddles on the aft end of an engine could be effective in directing the engine's thrust. The experiments showed promise, and he soon convinced the Navy to support further tests with Inconel steel paddles attached to the engine nozzles of both an F-14 model in Langley's 16-foot transonic tunnel and on a full-scale F-14 fighter. The flight tests were conducted at the Navy's flight test center at Patuxent River Naval Air Station, Maryland, and involved only a single paddle behind each engine nozzle for increased yaw control. The tests were limited, but were important for two reasons. First, the positive test results with the F-14 increased interest in thrust-vectoring for yaw control of an aircraft. And second, Lacey's work had given other researchers confidence in his relatively low-cost paddle approach to testing thrust-vectoring. Both the F-18 High Alpha Research

[13] "Final Report for Period October 1984 to 31 August 1991," STOL/Maneuver Technology Demonstrator, Volume 1, Executive Summary, WL-TR-91-3080, 30 September 1991; Chambers, *Partners in Freedom*, 159-163. Collection, 12; Chambers, *Partners in Freedom*, 215-218.

[14] Chambers, *Partners in Freedom*, 122; Chambers, interviewed by author, 15 August 2001.

[12] Chambers, *Partners in Freedom*, 44; Chambers, interviewed by author, 15 August 2001.

The X-31, a joint German-American project, employed an original airframe. Two aircraft were built and flown. Visible in the head-on view of the X-31 are several distinguishing features of the aircraft, among them the fore planes, or canards, and the strakes aft of the fuselage. Apparent is the absence of any horizontal stabilizer. The canards and the thrust-vectoring paddles compensated for this absence in addition to providing a high degree of maneuverability.

Vehicle (HARV) and the X-31 research aircraft used modified versions of Lacey's paddle system to create cost-effective multi-axis thrust-vectoring systems.[15]

The X-31

While Navy officials were investigating methods for reducing stall-spin losses in F-14s, several other research projects were beginning to evaluate thrust-vectoring as a way to increase fighter aircraft agility, by allowing the use of extremely high-angle-of-attack maneuvers in combat. In 1973, NASA and the Air Force began a research project to test several new technologies aimed at enhancing the maneuverability of future fighter planes. The goal of the Highly Maneuverable Aircraft Technology (HiMAT) program was to design a remotely piloted research vehicle whose performance would be 100% better than that of standard 1973-era fighters. Rockwell International was awarded the contract to build two of the scale model HiMAT vehicles, both of which were flown at Dryden from 1979 through 1983.

The original HiMAT design called for a two-dimensional thrust-vectoring nozzle, but cost con-siderations forced elimination of the nozzle in the final design. Even without thrust-vectoring, however, the HiMAT vehicles were highly successful for they achieved all the program goals, including sustained 8g turns at 25,000 feet.[16]

At the same time, interest in thrust-vectoring as a means of improving fighter aircraft maneuverability was also growing on the other side of the Atlantic. As early as the mid-1970s, Dr. Wolfgang Herbst, an engineer with the West German aircraft manufacturer Messerschmitt-Bölkow-Blohm (MBB), began arguing that new fighters needed the ability to maneuver in "post-stall," (PST) or high-angle-of-attack conditions in order to capitalize on the capabilities of new short-range missiles.

[15] "F-14/F-110 High Angle of Attack Flight Tests," SETP 32nd Symposium Proceedings, ISSN# 0742-3705, (Los Angeles, CA: October 1988), 24-40; Chambers, *Partners in Freedom*, 101-108; William P. Gilbert, interviewed by author, 13 August 2001; Joe Gera, interviewed by author, 8 August 2001; Chambers, interviewed by author, 15 August 2001.

[16] Richard P. Hallion and Michael H. Gorn, *On the Frontier: Experimental Flight at NASA Dryden* (Washington, D.C.: Smithsonian Books, 2003), 277; "Rollout," MBB Publication, 1 March 1990, DFRC Historical Reference Collection, 12; Chambers, *Partners in Freedom*, 215-218.

A series of manned and computer simulations conducted by the German Industrieanlagen Betriebsgesellschaft (IABG) and McDonnell Douglas in 1977 and 1978 showed that the ability to maneuver instantly and at slow speed could give a fighter significant advantage in firing short-range missiles. Encouraged by these results, Herbst wanted to build a research aircraft to prove the viability of a thrust-vectored fighter optimized for post-stall maneuvering, yet he knew MBB could not afford the cost of such a program on its own. By 1982, MBB had withdrawn from the Agile Combat Aircraft program (which later became the Experimental Aircraft Program, or EAP). Coincidentally, officials at Rockwell, where the B-1 bomber had only just been revived, were interested in broadening the company's horizons to mitigate future program cancellations.

In 1982, engineers at the two companies began discussing the possibility of working together on a post-stall research and flight demonstrator they dubbed the Super Normal Attitude Kinetic Enhancement (SNAKE) program. After a series of briefings in 1983, the U.S. Defense Advanced Research Projects Agency (DARPA) approved funds for a joint study of the concept. In 1986, the Nunn-Quayle initiative, which created funding for international armament programs, allowed the study to proceed to the next step: development of a full-fledged international flight research program. In May of that year, Rockwell, MBB, DARPA, and the West German Ministry of Defense (GMOD) signed an official agreement to construct and flight test a purpose-built research aircraft to investigate the tactical utility of thrust-vectoring and post-stall maneuvering. The project was designated the Enhanced Fighter Maneuverability (EFM) flight research program. In February 1987 the EFM design, which blended characteristics from early ideas developed by both Rockwell and MBB, received its official designation as the X-31A, making it the first international "X-plane" program.[17]

The F-18 High Alpha Research Vehicle

In the course of research efforts throughout the late 1970s and early 1980s, NASA engineers began talking among themselves about some of the difficulties

NASA 840, the F-18 HARV, flying over the Mojave Desert. Sporting both the ANSET nose strakes and the thrust-vectoring paddles, the jet also is heavily instrumented with bands of sensors running laterally and horizontally along the wings, fuselage and vertical tail surfaces.

[17] Rollout," MBB Publication, 5-17; "The X-31: The First International US/German Experimental Program," Deutsche Aerospace Publication, undated, DFRC Historical Reference Collection; Chambers, *Partners in Freedom*, 215-219.

posed by this new realm of high-alpha, post-stall flight. Researchers knew that the aerodynamic phenomena that occurred in those conditions were complex and not

The ACTIVE F-15 in flight over California's Antelope Valley, near Edwards Air Force Base. The type of exhaust nozzle on the aircraft was dubbed the "pitch/yaw balanced beam nozzle" and allowed axisymmetric thrust-vectoring up to 20 degrees in any direction.

easily extrapolated from known data at lower angles of attack. And since aircraft had not been capable of reaching or sustaining flight in those conditions prior to the development of thrust-vectoring, there was little solid flight data with which to validate theoretical computer or wind tunnel models.

In 1983, representatives from Langley, the NASA Ames Research Center, Moffett Field, California, and Dryden combined forces and approached Bill Aiken, head of the Office of Aeronautics and Space Technology (OAST) at NASA Headquarters, about conducting an integrated research program to investigate the aerodynamic phenomena associated with high-alpha flight. The program they proposed would include wind tunnel tests, computational fluid dynamics work, and flight tests with a high-performance aircraft modified with thrust-vectoring capability to allow sustained high-alpha flight. Managers at NASA Headquarters were initially skeptical about the costs of such a program. But Dave Lacey's external paddle approach to thrust-vectoring conducted at the Navy's David

Taylor Model Basin offered a proven and relatively inexpensive method of achieving thrust-vectoring on a full-scale aircraft, and the HATP was ultimately approved. The NASA team obtained an F-18 aircraft from the Navy to use for the program, and NASA's F-18 HARV made its first flight in April 1987.[18]

The F-15 Advanced Controls Technology for Integrated Vehicles (ACTIVE)

The paddle approach to thrust-vectoring used in both the X-31 and F-18 HARV aircraft was relatively simple and cost-effective. But the paddles added a tremendous amount of weight to the back end of the aircraft and were not practical for a production-type thrust-vectoring system. So while the X-31 and F-18 HARV programs began investigating the dynamics and potential tactical benefits of thrust-vectoring using the low-cost paddle method, both Pratt & Whitney and General Electric were working on designs for production-type axisymmetric, gimballing engine nozzles that would allow much more streamlined and efficient vectoring of engine exhaust.

As this work progressed, two additional flight research programs began investigating the use of this "second-generation" thrust-vectoring nozzle technology.

[18] "F-18 #840 HARV Flight Chronology," DFRC Historical Reference Collection; "High Alpha Technology Program (HATP) Program Plan, 19 March 1990, DFRC Historical Reference Collection; Chambers, *Partners in Freedom*, 38-40; Gilbert, interviewed by author, 13 August 2001; Chambers, interviewed by author, 15 August 2001.

The first, the Multi-Axis Thrust Vectoring (MATV) program, was a joint effort of the U.S. Air Force, General Dynamics, and General Electric. The MATV was a limited program that involved modifying an F-16 research plane with a General Electric axisymmetric thrust-vectoring nozzle and conducting a narrow, six-month flight test program with the aircraft. The focus of the F-16 MATV program was strictly on the tactical benefits a thrust-vectoring nozzle of that type could give a fighter aircraft. The six-month flight test program took place in 1993, and showed that thrust-vectoring could offer fighter pilots meaningful tactical advantages. But the program did not evaluate the actual efficiency or dynamics of the thrust-vectoring system used on the aircraft; some of those questions were addressed by a second flight research program involving Pratt & Whitney's competing axisymmetric thrust-vectoring nozzle design.[19]

While General Electric worked with General Dynamics on the F-16 MATV program, officials at Pratt & Whitney began a dialogue with NASA, the Air Force Research Laboratories, and the McDonnell Douglas Phantom Works about conducting a flight research program that incorporated its own thrust-vectoring nozzle design. Pratt & Whitney's primary objective was to flight validate its Pitch/Yaw Balance Beam Nozzle (P/YBBN). NASA, however, saw in this effort an opportunity to investigate both the specific propulsive dynamics of thrust-vectoring as well as the behavior and dynamics of thrust-vectoring across a much wider spectrum of the fighter aircraft envelope. In the resulting research program (dubbed ACTIVE), two Pratt & Whitney F100-PW-229 turbofans modified with the P/YBBN nozzles were installed in the highly modified S/MTD F-15 that had demonstrated two-dimensional thrust-vectoring for the Air Force a few years earlier. The aircraft, the sixth pre-production F-15 and the first two-seat F-15, was a unique vehicle and an ideal testbed for a more complex thrust-vectoring flight research project. Because it had been used for the S/MTD program, the aircraft already had

been modified with a quadruplex digital flight control and engine control system, an advanced glass cockpit design, integrated, digital flight test instrumentation, and a pair of variable canards.

The F-15 ACTIVE flight tests began in 1995 and ran through the summer of 1999. The four-year research effort produced a wide range of valuable information about not only the dynamics of thrust-vectoring but also the dynamics and behavior of the Pratt & Whitney F100-PW-229 engine. And a variety of new technologies descended the program, including methodologies for making real-time measurements of thrust and vector forces.[20]

[19] A two-dimensional vectoring nozzle allows thrust to be directed in two axes, typically up and down. Axisymmetric vectoring can direct exhaust in a 360 degree arc by rotating the entire nozzle in any given direction. The paddles on the HARV and the X-31 were incapable of true axisymmetric vectoring, although in coordination they could approximate axisymmetric thrust.

[20] Larry Walker, et. al, "ACTIVE F-15 Flight Research Program, paper presented at the SETP 40th Annual Symposium (Beverly Hills, CA, September 1996); Joseph E. Sweeney and Major Michael A. Gerzanics, "F-16 Multi-Axis Thrust Vectoring Program," SETP Thirty-seventh Symposium Proceedings, ISSN# 0742-3705, (Beverly Hills, CA, September 1993), 165-196; Joseph E. Sweeney and Major Michael A. Gerzanics, "F-16 MATV Envelope Expansion," SETP Thirty-eighth Symposium Proceedings, ISSN# 0742-3705, (Beverly Hills, CA, September 1993), 285-300; P. Doane, et. al, "F-15 ACTIVE: A Flexible Propulsion Integration Testbed," paper presented at the 30th AIAA/ASME/SAE/ASEE Joint Propulsion Conference, (Indianapolis, IN, June 27-29, 1994), 1-2; Gerard Schkolnik, interviewed by author, 30 March 2001; Roger Bursey, "The F-15 ACTIVE Aircraft 'The Next Step,' final draft of paper for AIAA publication, 6 July 1995, DFRC Historical Reference Collection; Schkolnik and Smolka, "F-15 Advanced Control Technology for Integrated Vehicles," paper presented at the Royal Aeronautical Society's 1999 Fighter Conference (England, 30 September 1999), from Gerard Schkolnik's personal files.

Chapter Two

The High Alpha Technology Program/ F-18 High Alpha Research Vehicle

Of the three multi-axis thrust-vectoring research programs flown at Dryden in the 1980s and 1990s, the High Alpha Technology Program (HATP) came closest to being a traditional NASA flight research effort. While the program involved a certain amount of partnering with industry and the military to obtain and modify the F-18 Hornet aircraft used in the program, it was predominantly an internal NASA research effort. The HATP was also a grassroots program that originated with NASA engineers, and involved multiple research disciplines and NASA centers. In addition, program objectives focused on advancing the general state of knowledge and technology, as opposed to the X-31 program, for example, which focused more on demonstrating some of the practical and tactical applications of the technology.

The HATP was conceived in the early 1980s, when representatives from several NASA research centers began discussing the various problems associated with flight at high angles of attack and the potential offered by multi-axis thrust-vectoring. Although military aircraft development programs regularly evaluated the behavior of aircraft at high angles of attack, the aerodynamics involved in that realm of flight were not well understood. NASA had conducted various high-alpha wind tunnel and simulation experiments, but there was little actual flight data available because aircraft lacked the ability to actually fly long enough at high angles of attack for data to be collected. In addition, engineers knew that the behavior of airflow and air pressures at high angles of attack was non-linear and complex, making it hard to extrapolate or model with confidence from existing data derived at lower angles of attack.

Yet the three-dimensional thrust-vectoring technology investigated in piloted simulations and wind tunnel experiments held tremendous potential for improving this situation. The military was primarily interested in thrust-vectoring as a means of enhancing the safety and maneuverability of fighters. At the same time, NASA engineers saw the technology as a means to significant aeronautical research. By making possible sustained flight at high angles of attack, they would be able to collect actual flight data from a realm they had been able to explore only in wind tunnels. Furthermore, coordinated efforts among several NASA centers would enable them to conduct parallel experiments in wind tunnels, computer simulations, and actual flight, allowing them to correlate the data. Such an effort would greatly enhance the accuracy of both wind tunnel and computer models and predictions of aircraft behavior at high angles of attack.

In addition, the process of developing a working multi-axis thrust-vectoring system for a research aircraft would provide NASA and industry engineers an opportunity to experiment with specific flight and engine control software and hardware necessary to make an integrated thrust-vectoring system work. Industry engineers would then have valuable tools, information, and flight-proven concepts available to them in the event the military's future needs called for fighters with multi-axis thrust-vectoring capability.

In 1983, Joe Chambers, Ken Szalai, and Roy Pressley presented a proposal for an integrated, multi-disciplinary high-alpha research program to Bill Aiken, head of NASA's Office of Aeronautics and Space Technology (OAST). Their proposal called for a coordinated effort involving their respective NASA research centers—Langley, Dryden, and Ames-Moffett—as well as NASA Lewis research center. At the time, Chambers was an assistant division chief at Langley Research Center who had been instrumental in developing previous high-alpha research efforts there, and Szalai was head of research at what was then the Ames-Dryden Flight Research Facility. Pressley was a division chief in the Aerodynamics Division of what was then the Ames-Moffett Research Center. Research tools would include computer models, wind tunnel tests, and flight research with a full-scale, thrust-vectoring-equipped aircraft, and the research would include experiments in aerodynamics, propulsion, advanced flight controls, and pilot/vehicle interfaces.

Aiken liked the idea and asked the three to present it to several different NASA advisory committees. The proposal was well received, although there was concern about the potential cost of such a program. Some feared that a research effort requiring the development of a thrust-vectoring engine for an aircraft seemed too expensive to justify. But Chambers, Szalai, and Pressley argued that it wasn't necessary to develop an entirely new engine in order to give a research aircraft thrust-vectoring capability. While the cumbersome aft-end paddle system used by Dave Lacey and the U.S. Navy wouldn't be practical for production aircraft, the paddles could be added to an existing fighter plane to create a workable thrust-vectoring system at relatively low cost. After numerous presentations and discussions, the HATP proposal was approved.

The overall objectives of the HATP, according to the program's initial flight test plan, were "to develop technology to permit safe, agile and controllable flight up to very high angles of attack, without catastrophic changes in forces and moments on the vehicle … to coordinate agency expertise and resources in an effective program that … permits exploitation of the high-angle-of-attack environment with maximum tactical effectiveness and safety."[1] Langley and Ames-Moffett were to take primary responsibility for the computational and wind tunnel aspects, Lewis was to take the lead on propulsion research, and Ames-Dryden was to head up flight research activities. All these efforts would be coordinated and supervised by a steering committee made up of representatives from the four centers, and management of funds allocated to the program would be shared among Langley, Dryden, and Lewis. Initially envisioned as a five-year project, with responsibility for the various research aspects shared among the four NASA aeronautics research centers, so rich was the research nature of the program that it lasted 12 years.

The program was a complex organizational structure that could easily have been plagued by turf battles. Looking back on the experience, researchers involved in the project agree that the various centers worked extremely well together throughout the program. Regardless of which center representative headed the steering committee, researchers felt that funds and resources were allocated fairly to different centers as workload and costs fluctuated throughout different phases of the program. From a management perspective, part of the reason the program worked so smoothly may have been that it began as an inter-center, grassroots effort. Managers and engineers at the centers decided they wanted to work together before the program or funding was ever approved. In addition, the program's multi-disciplinary nature served to eliminate any argument over whether experiments should be conducted on a computer, in a wind tunnel, or in actual flight; HATP experiments were conducted in all three areas. The multi-center, multi-disciplinary nature of the program also meant that personnel regularly traveled among the different NASA centers for briefings and meetings, giving them an appreciation for the strengths and challenges of the partners in the research effort. Today most of the researchers involved in the HATP effort continue to describe it as a model inter-center research effort.[2]

Even before the program had been approved, Chambers, Pressley, and Szalai began looking for a suitable aircraft for the flight portion of their proposed high-alpha research program. Because they knew they had to keep project costs as low as possible, the researchers ruled out building an entirely new research aircraft almost from the start. They considered both the forward-swept-wing X-29, which had recently emerged from the Grumman factory, and a modified McDonnell Douglas F-15. But in the end, they decided that the best candidate would be a McDonnell Douglas F-18 Hornet, the Navy's newest fighter jet.[3]

The F-18 was particularly well suited for a high-alpha research program for several reasons. Since it was a production aircraft, a wealth of flight data about its behavior and characteristics already existed. It also had a fully digital flight-control system, which was

---

[1] "F-18 High Angle of Attack Flight Test Plan," Ames Research Center and Dryden Flight Research Facility Document HA 86-301, November 1986, 2.

[2] Donald Gatlin, interviewed by Lane E. Wallace, 14 August 2001; Joseph R. Chambers, interviewed by Lane E. Wallace, 15 August 2001; William P. Gilbert, interviewed by Lane E. Wallace, 13 August 2001; Robert Meyer, interviewed by Lane E. Wallace, 9 August 2001.

[3] The official designation for the Hornet is now an F/A-18, denoting its dual role as a fighter/attack aircraft. But the designation was simply F-18 until 1984. As NASA's High Alpha Research Vehicle (HARV) was built in 1980, it referred to it as most of the HATP documents did—simply as an F-18.

necessary in order to make a transparent, integrated thrust-vectoring system possible. In addition, the F-18 had demonstrated good controllability at relatively high angles of attack (up to 55 degrees), and its General Electric F404-GE-400 afterburning, turbofan engines performed well in that region. One of the many problems with slow-speed, high-alpha flight was that it could disturb airflow into engine inlets to such an extent that the engines stalled, leading to a loss of control. The F-18 also had excellent spin-recovery characteristics, which would be important in researching a realm of flight in which a loss of control would be likely to put an aircraft into a spin. Furthermore, the F-18 suffered peculiar aerodynamic phenomena such as wing rock and tail buffeting that researchers were eager to study. Not coincidentally, these aerodynamic idiosyncrasies seemed to result from disturbed or vortical airflow at higher angles of attack.

The Navy was very receptive to the idea of supporting a high-alpha research program and offered to loan NASA an early production model F-18 for the effort. But Chambers asked instead for the pre-production F-18 that had been used to conduct high-alpha and spin testing for the design during its development phase. The NASA team wanted that particular F-18 because it already was outfitted with a back-up emergency power system and spin-recovery parachute–important elements for a high-alpha research vehicle that would cost several million dollars to add to any other aircraft. Unfortunately, that particular aircraft, which had been mothballed after completing the spin-testing program, had been used as a spare parts vehicle for other F-18s at the Navy's Patuxent River, Maryland, flight test facilities. Its condition was more a collection of parts than a complete airplane.

"Have you seen the airplane lately?" an incredulous Navy officer asked Chambers upon hearing the request.

Chambers had, but he insisted that his group wanted the airplane anyway. So in October 1984, F-18 Ship Number F6, Bureau Number 160780, was shipped to Dryden by truck "in a bushel basket," as Langley researcher William Gilbert described it. The aircraft had been cannibalized so extensively during its time in storage that it was missing more than 400 parts. To assist in the monumental task of rebuilding the airframe the Navy also sent two other pre-production

F-18s–Ship Number F1 and Ship Number F9–for spare parts to help NASA piece together a single, flyable High Alpha Research Vehicle (HARV).[4]

By the fall of 1985, NASA headquarters had approved the HATP, and work began on restoring the F-18 to flight status. It took more than a year to rebuild the airplane, with the equivalent of 46 people working full time on the project. The transformation from what amounted to little more than a pile of scrap metal to a sleek, state-of-the-art research aircraft was so profound that NASA researchers dubbed the airplane the "Silk Purse," in defiance of the old saying that it was impossible to "make a silk purse from a sow's ear." The team even painted "Silk Purse" in gold script just under the cockpit on the F-18 HARV fuselage, where it remains. Finally, by the end of March 1987, the F-18 HARV was cleared for flight, and on 2 April 1987, the "Silk Purse," with its new tail number of NASA 840, took to the skies for the first time in its new research role.[5]

The High Alpha Technology Program: Phase I

The HATP research effort was initially divided into two phases. In the first, researchers sought to collect baseline aerodynamic data on the F-18 at intermediate and high angles of attack (up to 55 degrees alpha) without thrust-vectoring capability. This data would be used for comparison with wind tunnel and computational predictions, and to develop new methods and criteria for high-alpha flight. The second phase would focus on implementing the thrust-vectoring system and

[4] Chambers, interviewed by Lane E. Wallace, 15 August 2001; "Navy/NASA Loan Agreement For F-18 Aircraft," document, 21 May 1986, DFRC Historical Reference Collection; Gilbert, interviewed by Lane E. Wallace, 13 August 2001; Chambers, *Partners in Freedom*, 38-39; Brad Flick, interviewed by Lane E. Wallace, 22 August 2001.

[5] "F-18 840 Chronology," part of documentation supporting Flight Request for Flight No. 1-2 of F-18 tail number 840, 13 March 1987, DFRC Historical Reference Collection; "Flight Report, Flights 1-3," Memo, From Donald H. Gatlin to OP/Chief, Dryden Aeronautical Projects Office, 29 April 1987, DFRC Historical Reference Collection; "F-18 #840 HARV Flight Chronology," undated document, DFRC Historical Reference Collection.

collecting data from whatever envelope expansion a thrust-vectoring system enabled. All this was to validate wind tunnel and computational predictions and to develop new methods and criteria for extreme flight envelope. A third research phase was eventually added that incorporated additional experiments in advanced control concepts in the high-alpha realm.[6]

Throughout all three phases of the program flight research was integrated with parallel or complementary experiments in piloted simulations and wind tunnels, and with computational models and predictions. When the HATP began, computational models of the flows over an F-18 at high angles of attack had never been made. One of the first successes in the program, then, was finding a way to create that type of baseline

currently in the wind tunnels at Langley and Ames (engineers at Ames even put a full-scale F-18 in the center's 80-by-120-foot wind tunnel for some experiments). And while piloted simulations (using models created from previous CFD and wind tunnel work) were used to give researchers and pilots an idea of what to expect before actually flying the F-18 HARV, actual flight data was then fed back into the simulation models to make those more accurate. As a result, the simulations became more refined, with greater benefit not only to future designers, but to the pilots and researchers involved in the HARV program.

This flexibility and integrated cooperation among researchers was one of the most distinctive characteristics of the HATP. Research results were shared among

Dye flow tests conducted before modifying the nose with adjustable strakes. The patterns of weeping glycol-based dye illustrate airflow over the fuselage at certain points while the aircraft was at high angles of attack, in this instance 30 degrees AoA.

computational model, a remarkable feat that computational fluid dynamics (CFD) researchers at Langley and Ames accomplished in a little over a year. The F-18 HARV flight data was then used to refine that model.

To verify and refine wind tunnel predictions, flight data from the F-18 HARV also was compared to data collected from identical experiments conducted con-

the different disciplines and continually fed back into the computer and wind tunnel models being used to advance the program. Indeed, this continual feedback

[6] "F-18 High Angle-of-Attack Flight Test Plan," HA 86-301, Ames Research Center, Dryden Flight Research Facility, November 1986, 2; "F-18 High Angle-of-Attack Flight Test Plan," HA 86-301 Revision A, Ames Research Center, Dryden Flight Research Facility, August 1987, 2.

and cooperation, and the flexibility and progress they fostered, were among the reasons for the HATP effort's success.[7]

Phase I:
Aircraft Modifications

Because the first phase of the research did not require thrust-vectoring, NASA technicians and researchers initially made relatively few major modifications to the F-18 HARV. The F-18's wingtip launching rails were replaced with wingtip camera pods and air data sensors, and extensive internal instrumentation was incorporated into the airplane. The instrumentation and systems on the F-18 HARV varied, however, depending on which research experiments were being conducted. As a result, the configuration changed somewhat even during the first phase of the flight research. The aircraft was outfitted with two telemetry systems capable of simultaneously transmitting video from any two of the aircraft's five video cameras (data from the remaining three was recorded on board) as well as 700 measurements, including over 500 individual surface pressures. The F-18 also was outfitted with two 35mm still cameras. Although the aircraft initially carried a typical flight test noseboom with which to record air data, researchers knew that at high angles of attack forebody airflows played a critical role in aircraft control, and the noseboom would interfere with those flows. So wingtip air data probes were developed in order that the noseboom could be removed as flight research progressed. Removing the noseboom created space for an experimental flush air data system (FADS) to be installed and tested in the aircraft's nose.

In addition, technicians modified the F-18 HARV with a system that emitted an evaporative propylene glycol monomethyl ether (PGME) dye to help trace and visualize attached airflow over the aircraft's forebody. The dye was emitted through pressure ports on the F-18's forebody and the leading edge extension (LEX)–a fairing that helped blend the Hornet's wing into the forward part of the fuselage–and dried in place, allowing researchers on the ground to analyze airflow after the plane landed. Because the PGME was pumped out of pressure ports, flow visualization experiments had to be completed on flights separate from those on which experiments requiring pressure measurements were conducted.

In order for the PGME to have a chance to leave an accurate record of flows at a particular condition, however, the pilot had to hold the plane steady at a precise test point for 75 to 90 seconds, a challenging task at some high-alpha conditions. To assist pilots in accomplishing this and other tasks, researchers outfitted the HARV with something called a "Remotely Augmented Vehicle," or RAV, capability. This system used a standard aircraft instrument that ordinarily displayed guidance cues for following an airport's instrument landing system (ILS) and modified it to give HARV pilots guidance cues for hitting specific test points. The system telemetered information about the plane's attitude and location to the ground and then back to the plane identifying how much the attitude, altitude, bank angle, etc., would need to be changed in order for the pilot to be "on target" for the next test point. The guidance cues were then displayed on the ILS instrument. If the two "needles" on the instrument were centered, the pilot had the plane exactly where it needed to be for the correct data to be collected.[8]

Additional instrumentation and flow visualization systems developed for Phase I HARV flights included a smoke-generating system that allowed researchers to observe detached airflows and vortices emanating from the aircraft's forebody and leading-edge extensions at high angles of attack. The smoke-generating system consisted of 12 cartridges capable of emitting smoke for 20-40 seconds each through four ports in the F-18's nose section. A rotating rake instrument with 16 probes also was fabricated and installed on the F-18's LEX for several flights. The rake recorded detailed pressure measurements, velocity, and flow direc-

---

[7] Chambers, interviewed by Lane E. Wallace, 15 August 2001.

[8] Albion H. Bowers, "F-18 High Alpha Research Vehicle: A 1995 Overview," draft, from Al Bowers personal files; Meyer, interviewed by Lane E. Wallace, 9 August 2001; Ed Schneider, interviewed by Lane E. Wallace, 10 August 2001; David F. Fisher, et. al, "Summary of In-flight Flow Visualization Obtained From the NASA High Alpha Research Vehicle," NASA Technical Memorandum TM-101734, January 1991, 3-4.

tion data from the airflow streaming past the LEX, helping researchers map and better understand the LEX and forebody vortices. Additional Phase I flights used nylon and wool "tufts" and "flow cones" on the wings, vertical tails, and forebody of the F-18 that were videotaped in flight to allow researchers to observe airflow patterns over those surfaces. Although the HARV aircraft had been selected as the research vehicle because it had a spin-recovery chute and emergency battery power system, technicians did not actually reinstall these systems on the vehicle until the end of the first research phase, in preparation for the higher-risk thrust-vectoring phase.[9]

Phase I:
Experiments

In the first phase of the F-18 HARV flight experiments, researchers sought to explore various aerodynamic phenomena of the aircraft at intermediate and high angles of attack. Researchers knew that the complex airflows that developed along the forebody of a fighter aircraft played an increasingly important role in its behavior as angle of attack increased. The F-18 (and F-16) designs also incorporated leading-edge extensions–fairings that stretched forward along the aircraft's forebody

from the leading edge of the wing, helping blend the wing into the fuselage. These fairings actually help create a phenomenon known as "vortex lift" which enhances the aircraft's performance at moderate and high angles of attack. But the exact characteristics and behavior of these leading-edge vortices were not well understood and were difficult to predict, especially when combined with the complex vortices that researchers knew were coming off the aircraft forebody.

The vortex flows off the F-18's forebody and leading-edge extensions seemed to create two other problems: a phenomenon known as "wing rock," and a harsh buffeting of the Hornet's twin vertical tails at high angles of attack. Wing rock was a degradation of lateral stability and control that seemed to occur between 35- and 45-degree angles of attack. The wings would rock without any control input even as the pilot tried to hold the aircraft steady at those angles of attack. The tail vibration that F-18s also experienced at high angles of attack was severe enough to cause structural fatigue on the Navy's fleet F-18s. A relatively small fence on the LEX near the wing root, tested in wind tunnels at Langley and McDonnell Douglas, mitigated the problem and had been installed on all F-18C/D aircraft. But the exact dynamics causing the problem were still not well understood.[10]

To gain a better understanding of these phenomena, HATP researchers used various combinations of PGME dye, tufts, smoke, the rotating LEX rake, and other pressure measurements. By tufting the vertical tails of the F-18 and examining the vortices coming off the forebody and LEX with the smoke-generating system, for example, engineers were able to map the behavior of the airflows causing the tail-buffeting problem and locate both the tightly wound LEX vortex and the position of the vortex bursting that had created the anomaly. HATP researchers also investigated the impact of the McDonnell Douglas-installed LEX fences on

[9] Albion H. Bowers, et. al, "An Overview of the NASA F-18 High Alpha Research Vehicle," NASA Technical Memorandum 4772 (Edwards, Ca, 1996), 5-13; "HARV Research Equipment," viewgraph, undated, DFRC Historical Reference Collection; Bowers, "F-18 High Alpha Research Vehicle,"; Chambers, interviewed by Lane E. Wallace, 15 August 2001; Gilbert, interviewed by Lane E. Wallace, 13 August 2001; "High Alpha Technology Program (HATP) Plan," program plan, 19 March 1990, DFRC Historical Reference Collection, 1-2, 24-28; John H. Del Frate and Fanny A. Zuniga, "In-flight Flow Field Analysis on the NASA F-18 High Alpha Research Vehicle with Comparisons to Ground Facility Data," paper, AIAA-90-0231, presented at the American Institute of Aeronautics and Astronautics 28th Aerospace Sciences meeting (Reno, NV: 8 – 11 January 1990), 2-3; David F. Fisher, et. al, "Summary of In-Flight Flow Visualization Obtained From the NASA High Alpha Research Vehicle," NASA Technical Memorandum TM-101734, January 1991, 1-4; D. Richwine and D. Fisher, "In-flight Leading-Edge Extension Vortex Flow-Field Survey Measurements on a F-18 Aircraft at High Angle of Attack," AIAA paper AIAA-91-3248, presented at the AIAA 9th Applied Aerodynamics Conference (Baltimore, MD: 23-25 September 1991), 346-347.

[10] Bowers, "F-18 High Alpha Research Vehicle: A 1995 Overview,"; David F. Fisher, et. al, "Summary of In-Flight Flow Visualization Obtained From the NASA High Alpha Research Vehicle," 1-7; Chambers, Partners in Freedom, 40; "F-18 High Angle-of-Attack Flight Test Plan," HA 86-301 Revision A, Ames Research Center, Dryden Flight Research Facility, August 1987, 2-6.

The contents of a smoke canister stream from tiny ports around the cockpit, providing engineers with evidence of airflow characteristics at high angles of attack. Tufts of yarn attached to the aircraft's surface also show airflow patterns. Chase planes prove indispensable in instances like this since they bring back still images and motion pictures of the test vehicle that allow engineers on the ground a chance to see things in ways that would otherwise be impossible. These tests were conducted before the F-18 had been modified.

the vortices disturbing the vertical tail, both in wind tunnel experiments and in flight with the HARV. The results gave engineers a much clearer picture of how the fences restructured the vortices and how, in turn, that mitigated the impact on the vertical tails.

The flow visualization experiments also showed researchers why the F-18 had a wing rock problem between 35- and 45-degree angles of attack. While changes in disturbed air flowing over the vertical tails in that region of the flight envelope seemed to be a contributing factor in creating wing rock, the HATP research indicated that the primary cause of the phenomenon was interaction between the F-18's

LEX and forebody vortices.[11]

Project engineers also were interested in investigating the flow dynamics and vortices coming off the HARV forebody. Several pressure and flow experiments were conducted in an attempt to characterize the turbulent and laminar flow that might occur in that area. One set of experiments,

[11] Fisher, et. al, "Summary of In-Flight Flow Visualization Obtained From the NASA High Alpha Research Vehicle," 1-8; Gary E. Erickson, "Wind Tunnel Investigation of Vortex Flows on F-18 Configuration at Subsonic Through Transonic Speeds," NASA Technical Paper 3111, December 1991, 1-2, 18-19; "F-18 – What We Learned," Dave Fisher email message to Lane Wallace, 27 August 2001, with comments by Dan Banks, Bob Hall, Jim Luckring and Dan Murri.

conducted at various points throughout the HARV flight program, involved putting "grit strips" on the aircraft forebody to create a predictable and controllable flow-separation point for exploring turbulent flow characteristics. But without the strips, the PGME flow-visualization experiments illustrated that there was an unexpected amount of laminar flow along the F-18 forebody–a phenomenon that wind tunnel tests had not predicted. This new piece of information helped create a more accurate picture of the aerodynamic characteristics of an F-18 at high angles of attack which, in turn, gave engineers the ability to better predict the in-flight behavior of other new or high-performance aircraft designs.[12]

Flow visualization was not the only type of research conducted with the F-18 HARV during Phase I flights, however. While aerodynamic researchers were focusing on flow visualization experiments, others were conducting flight experiments to evaluate the handling qualities and agility of the F-18 at high angles of attack and gather data for the purposes of what is known as parameter estimation, or identification.

Parameter identification is a technique developed by researchers to help predict an aircraft's behavior based on the time-honored physics equation of F = MA, or Force = Mass x Acceleration. Researchers know the mass of an aircraft model in wind tunnel experiments and can directly measure a given force exerted on that model with a specific control-surface deflection or configuration. Using those two pieces of information, they solve for the third variable, acceleration (the aircraft's response to force exerted on it by specific control inputs). With that data, a simulation model can be built to predict how the airplane would respond to those forces in actual flight.

But researchers solve the equation differently in actual flight. Through careful documentation of the amount and distribution of an aircraft's weight, its mass can be accurately calculated. Then, extensive instrumentation of an aircraft allows engineers to measure the aircraft's actual response or acceleration to a series of very precise flight maneuvers. From those two pieces of information, researchers can then solve for the force that must be exerted on the aircraft to produce that degree of acceleration. This is the process in flight research

called parameter identification or estimation.

Determining and verifying the accuracy of these specific aerodynamic coefficients is extremely important in order for engineers to be able to trust computer models and wind tunnel predictions for new aircraft designs. And in the complex realm of high-alpha flight, the validation offered by the F-18 HARV parameter identification experiments was just as important as the data on vortex and airflow behavior in both the refining of ground design tools and in bolstering designers' confidence in those tools, used for predicting high-alpha behavior.[13]

The HATP research did not immediately create solutions to any of the high-alpha phenomena or anomalies experienced by the F-18 and other high-performance aircraft. But the Phase I experiments with the F-18 HARV, conducted over the course of 101 flights from April 1987 to September 1989, helped develop tools for better visualization of aerodynamic flows, enabling researchers to better map and understand the complex airflows and vortices associated with high-alpha flight. Phase I experiments in both flow visualization and parameter identification also helped verify and refine wind tunnel and computational predictions in the high-alpha realm, increasing confidence in those design tools.

These experiments continued throughout the second and third phases of the F-18 HARV program, expanding the database into higher angles of attack and areas of advanced controls. As a result of this extensive and coordinated flight and ground research, engineers now have much better information on high-alpha aerodynamics available to them, as well as more accurate computer models and tools for designing future high-performance aircraft that can perform more safely and efficiently at high angles of attack.[14]

---

[12] Meyer, interviewed by Lane E. Wallace, 10 August 2001; Fisher, et. al, "Summary of In-Flight Flow Visualization Obtained from the NASA High Alpha Research Vehicle," 10-11.

[13] Bowers, interviewed by Lane E. Wallace, 29 March 2001; "F-18 Objective and Requirements Document" No. 1, 29 May 1987, and Document H, 5 August 1987, DFRC Historical Reference Collection.

[14] "F-18 #840 Flight Chronology," DFRC Historical Reference Collection.

The High Alpha Technology Program: Phase II

While Phase I experiments were being conducted on the F-18 HARV, the McDonnell Douglas Aircraft Company was working on the design of the thrust-vectoring system that would be added to the aircraft for Phase II flight experiments.

The primary goal of Phase II experiments was to explore the expanded high-alpha flight envelope made possible by the multi-axis thrust-vectoring system, both in terms of the aerodynamic phenomena that occurred there and the increased maneuverability that thrust-vectoring might foster. Using thrust-vectoring, the HARV was able to reach and sustain up to 70 degrees alpha, an angle of attack 15 degrees higher than is attainable with a stock F-18. But researchers also were interested in evaluating the agility and handling characteristics of a thrust-vectored aircraft in high-alpha flight. This phase of the HATP program also offered researchers the chance to explore and develop some of the technologies that would inevitably accompany a multi-axis thrust-vectoring system, such as new flight control laws and flight control systems.

Phase II: Aircraft Modifications

The design and fabrication of the F-18 HARV multi-axis thrust-vectoring system, which was patterned after the single-paddle thrust-vectoring system flight-tested on a Navy F-14 in the early 1980s, was contracted out to McDonnell Douglas in July 1987. The award was a logical one, since McDonnell Douglas had built the F-18 and therefore had intimate knowledge of the aircraft and its systems. The F-18 HARV thrust-vectoring system, installed on both of the aircraft's General Electric F404-GE-400 engines, featured three hydraulically actuated paddles, or "vanes," fabricated from Inconel, an extremely heat-resistant nickel alloy. The vanes were attached around the exhaust nozzles of each engine in place of the divergent portion of the engines' afterburner nozzles, and could move in an arc up to 25 degrees, resulting in 15 to 20 degrees of thrust-vectoring. Extra heat shielding was applied to prevent the hot, vectored exhaust gases from damaging other components at the rear of the aircraft. In order to keep the vanes from interfering with the aircraft's structure the two lower vanes of each nozzle were slightly smaller than the third, upper vane, and the vanes were unequally spaced around the nozzle. While these inconsistencies caused a slight asymmetry in the effectiveness of the thrust-vectoring, the system was judged to work well enough for research purposes.[15]

Indeed, the cost-effectiveness of the F-18 HARV thrust-vectoring system was based entirely on its short-term research role. The system was functional, and was hinged on a boilerplate design that was neither efficient nor designed for long-term use. The system, for one, was extremely heavy. The installation of the Thrust-vectoring Control System (TVCS) on the HARV increased the plane's weight by 2,200 pounds, leading program engineers to joke about the aircraft having "a ton of thrust-vectoring" on it.[16] The thrust-vectoring system added so much weight to the back of the plane that an additional 893 pounds of ballast had to be added to its nose to keep its center of gravity within limits. Between removing the divergent section of the F-18's afterburning nozzles and adding the extra weight to the airplane, the F-18 HARV was no longer able to achieve supersonic flight, a performance cost acceptable only in a research fighter aircraft.

The unusual weight distribution of the thrust-vectoring system at the aircraft's aft end, and the extra ballast in the F-18's nose, also meant that the aircraft's mass distribution now was rather like that of a heavy-ended dumbbell weight. This meant the aircraft might behave very differently than would a stock F-18, especially in a spin. So one of the first orders of business with the modified F-18 HARV was to complete a series of spin tests (or "yaw rate expansion" experiments, as they became known at Dryden) to ensure that the aircraft would have acceptable spin-recovery characteristics. The F-18's original spin-recovery chute was reinstalled before the Phase II flights began, as was the emergency battery power system.

Rather than integrate the thrust-vectoring system

---

[15] Bowers, et. al, "An overview of the NASA F-18 High Alpha Research Vehicle," 15-16; "NASA High Alpha Research Vehicle Thrust Vectoring System," undated viewgraph, from DFRC Historical Reference Collection.

[16] Chambers, interviewed by Lane E. Wallace, 15 August 2001; Gatlin, interviewed by Lane E. Wallace, 14 August 2001.

into the HARV basic flight control software, engineers designed the Research Flight Control System (RFCS) as a separate set of flight control laws that could be switched on and off during flight. This gave researchers greater flexibility and a wider safety margin in testing both the flight control software and the thrust-vectoring system. Use of the TVCS and RFCS was limited to a small portion of the F-18 HARV flight envelope. The system was set up, for example, to automatically disengage if the aircraft went below 15,000 feet or above 35,000 feet in altitude or above .7 Mach in speed, and flight restrictions called for the system never to be engaged during takeoff or landing.[17] By electing not to make the vectoring software flight-critical, the HATP team dramatically reduced the complexity of the flight control software required to operate the thrust-vectoring system. This, in turn, reduced the time needed to design the system, as well as its costs.

Designing the RFCS as an "add-on" rather than a flight-critical system had other advantages. For one, the pilot could switch off the RFCS and revert to the stock F-18 flight control software. The immediate benefit of this arrangement was that experimental

After painting, and now completely outfitted, the HARV is ready for flight. The paddles, hydraulic actuators and control box are clearly visible in the photograph. Without power, the hydraulically actuated paddles relax and hang loosely.

control laws could be tested in flight with less extensive ground testing and reviews than "Class A," or flight-critical software changes ordinarily required. For another, the single-string, "Class B" nature of the software meant that it was relatively easy for researchers to make changes in the RFCS and experiment with new control laws. In addition to broadening the scope of flight control research that could be conducted in the limited lifespan of the F-18 HARV program, this capability also allowed researchers to make rapid changes in the flight control software to respond to unexpected research results, making the HARV a much more productive research tool.[18]

To improve the HARV's ability to achieve precise data points at extremely high angles of attack, the aircraft also was equipped with something called the On Board Excitation System (OBES), a set of preprogrammed maneuvers integrated into the aircraft's flight control computer. In order to get exact data for parameter identification and comparison with wind tunnel and computational models, very precise and repeatable maneuvers were required from the aircraft. The thrust-vectoring system was expected to help stabilize the aircraft at high angles of attack but repeating maneuvers with pinpoint accuracy in that region of flight would still be extremely difficult for pilots. Using the OBES, however, pilots would simply select a particular maneuver, such as a "doublet," and push an "execute" button.[19] The OBES would then command the desired maneuver automatically, almost as if the maneuvers were being performed by an autopilot. Use of the system could also enable movement of a single control surface, allowing experimenters to isolate particular responses and collect specific data on particular parameters. The OBES system, which could command up to 31 combinations of surface-motion options, offered the advantage of reducing pilot workload while simultaneously producing extremely

precise and specific flight data for researchers on the ground.[20]

Simulation

Simulation has many uses in any flight research project. With varying degrees of sophistication, desktop, fixed base and motion, and "hardware-in-the-loop" simulations can be used for software development, pilot training, flight-test planning, and/or engineering development.

The HATP made extensive use of simulation at every stage, especially as one of the program's explicit goals was to correlate actual flight data with existing computer simulation models. But as the HARV flight research moved into the higher-risk and lesser-known realm of extremely high-alpha and thrust-vectored flight, simulation began to play an even more important role. In addition to helping researchers develop control laws for flight control software, simulations allowed pilots and researchers to ground test the function of the F-18's various components and modifications and examine how the HARV would behave with the added weight and control power of thrust-vectoring. Simulations also allowed researchers to explore potential flight anomalies that might be encountered in the expanded flight envelope, which included angles of attack never before achieved with an F-18 in flight.

Several types of simulation were used with the F-18 HARV flight program, from basic workstation "batch" simulation and various levels of hardware-in-the-loop simulations to the use of a full "Iron Bird." The Iron Bird in this case was a static F-18 aircraft modified to duplicate the HARV, including hydraulics and actuators for all control surfaces (except leading- and trailing-edge flaps), actual flight control and mission computers, and realistic avionics in a full-scale

[17]"F-18 High Angle of Attack Research Vehicle: Research Flight Control System Test Plan," 18 January 1991, DFRC Historical Reference Collection; Victoria Regenie, et. al, "The F-18 High Alpha Research Vehicle: A High-Angle-of-Attack Testbed Aircraft," AIAA paper AIAA-92-4121, presented at the 6th AIAA Biennial Flight Test Conference (Hilton Head Island, SC: 24-26 August, 1992), 5-7.

[18] Bowers, et. al, "An Overview of the NASA F-18 High Alpha Research Vehicle," 16-17; Schneider, interviewed by Lane E. Wallace, 10 August 2001.

[19] A "pulse" is when the pilot moves the control stick from neutral in one direction, and returns it to neutral without a pause. If, after completing a pulse, the pilot promptly moves the stick the opposite direction to an equal degree and returns it to neutral, it is a "doublet." Doublets are used to measure such features as hysteresis and time constants.

[20] Schneider, interviewed by Lane E. Wallace, 10 August 2001; Bowers, et. al, "An Overview of the NASA F-18 High Alpha Research Vehicle," 17, 24; Regenie, et. al, "The F-18 High Alpha Research," 7.

cockpit. The extensive use of realistic hardware in the Iron Bird system allowed researchers to check final system configurations before flight.[21]

Engineers at Langley and Ames also relied on various levels of simulation in developing flight control software, including the use of Langley's Differential Maneuvering Simulator (DMS). A dome simulator at the Patuxent River Naval Air Station also was used to evaluate the F-18 HARV response to various failures in the Thrust-vectoring Control System (TVCS).

Incorporating simulation into the research effort of the HATP had several benefits. By conducting simulation and wind tunnel experiments simultaneously with flight test, and by sharing a simulation database among different centers, discrepancies could be resolved and discoveries could be incorporated immediately. As a result, each simulation was more accurate than the last. Considering the extensive modifications to the F-18 HARV control system and the unknown aspects of the region of flight being explored, relatively few surprises or unexpected anomalies were encountered during flight. HARV researchers attribute this achievement largely to the extensive use of simulation throughout the project.[22]

Phase II:
Experiments

The first flight of the F-18 HARV with the thrust-vectoring system installed on the aircraft took place on 16 January 1991. The first flight in which thrust-vectoring was actually used on the F-18, however, was the 104th flight of the program, on 12 July 1991, with pilot Ed Schneider at the controls. The thrust-vectoring system was engaged for only a few minutes but the flight was momentous nonetheless, for it marked the first time an aircraft had utilized a three-dimensional,

or multi-axis, thrust-vectoring system in flight.[23]

The 36 flights following the July 1991 flight focused on thorough and careful expansion of the F-18 HARV envelope, including spin testing. Spins in the F-18 were of real concern to researchers for two reasons. First, the Phase II flights would take the HARV out of an F-18's conventional flight envelope. If for any reason the RFCS that controlled the aircraft's thrust-vectoring reverted to the standard F-18 control laws while the HARV was at an angle-of-attack beyond the normal control envelope, the plane could easily depart controlled flight and enter a spin. Second, although the standard F-18 had proven and acceptable spin-recovery characteristics, the altered weight and mass distribution resulting from the thrust-vectoring system could make the HARV behave very differently in a spin. But the researchers, and particularly the pilots slated to conduct HARV flights, still wanted to explore potential spin anomalies in a controlled flight experiment rather than encountering them by surprise.

As pilots and researchers who worked on the program tell it, Milt Thompson, who was chief engineer at Dryden and a former X-15 research pilot, was uncomfortable with the idea of intentionally spinning a high-performance, experimental aircraft. Thompson reportedly even placed a $100 wager with HARV pilots, betting they would have to "use the spin chute in anger" at least once during the program. So the HARV spin tests became euphemistically known as "yaw rate expansion" experiments, at least in official flight requests. These yaw rate expansion experiments were lively events; one pilot equated the experience with "being inside a washing machine." But even with all the HARV modifications the aircraft still had acceptable spin-recovery characteristics, and Thompson lost his bet; the F-18's emergency spin chute never had to be deployed in flight.[24]

---

[21] The first Iron Bird was a simple cruciform I-beam structure with reaction control motors at the ends of each arm. A pilot sat near the "nose " and activated the hydrogen peroxide rockets with a control stick.

[22] Regenie, et al, "The F-18 High Alpha Research Vehicle," 9-10; Bowers, et. al, "An Overview of the NASA F-18 High Alpha Research Vehicle," 18-19; Schneider, interviewed by Lane E. Wallace, 10 August 2001; Chambers, *Partners in Freedom*, 40; Meyer, interviewed by Lane E. Wallace, 9 August 2001; Gilbert, interviewed by Lane E. Wallace, 13 August 2001.

[23] "F-18 #840 Flight Chronology," DFRC Historical Reference Collection; Breck W. Henderson, "Dryden Completes First Flights of F-18 HARV with Thrust Vectoring, *Aviation Week & Space Technology*, 29 July 1991, 25; Schneider, interviewed by Lane E. Wallace, 10 August 2001; Bowers, "F-18 High Alpha Research Vehicle: A 1995 Overview."

[24] "HARV Tech Brief II-7," 14 July 1992, viewgraphs, DFRC Historical Reference Collection; Bowers, interviewed by Lane E. Wallace, 29 March 2001; Schneider, interview with Lane E. Wallace, Edwards, CA, 24 August 1995; Schneider, interviewed by Lane E. Wallace, 10 August 2001.

A bigger challenge facing the research pilots, as it turned out, was refueling the modified F-18 HARV in flight. The HARV RFCS, which incorporated the thrust-vectoring system, was activated only during experimental portions of the flight. For all other flight phases, HARV pilots used the stock F-18 flight control system, which had not been designed for the unusual weight and configuration of the HARV. The airframe modifications and the unusual distribution of weight resulted in considerable lag in the standard control response. This generally didn't pose a problem, even for takeoff and landing, but the aircraft proved difficult to maneuver with the accuracy required for in-flight refueling. It took Ed Schneider, the primary research pilot for the F-18 HARV, 45 minutes to refuel the aircraft on his first attempt. The pilots improved their technique over time, but refueling the F-18 HARV in flight remained a challenge throughout the flight program.[25]

Once the envelope expansion with the modified HARV had been completed, the next set of research experiments began. Phase II continued the aerodynamic and parameter identification experiments from Phase I, with data being collected from higher alphas. But flight-control research also became a much more important component during this phase of the program. Base, where the Dryden Flight Research Center is located.

Control Law Experiments

Among the goals of the HATP was to explore the flight control laws and software that would be necessary components of any production thrust-vectoring system. The first flight control laws flown with the HARV thrust-vectoring system were designed by McDonnell Douglas and Honeywell, but in the course of the HARV flights, no fewer than five sets of control laws, and five versions of one control law, were flown

on the airplane.[26]

Designing control laws for the F-18 HARV was particularly challenging because controlling an aircraft at high angles of attack was not only uncharted territory, it was also territory in which the aerodynamics changed dramatically in flight. Control laws needed flexible "gains" that would allow for the changing and non-linear aerodynamics of the high-alpha region.[27] However, one of the surprises researchers discovered through the HATP was that even though the aerodynamics of the high-alpha region were non-linear, flight control laws for high-alpha flight did not necessarily have to be non-linear. Through the various flight-control experiments on the HARV, researchers learned that it was possible to extend the flight characteristics pilots wanted at lower angles of attack, and the control laws necessary to produce those characteristics, into the high-alpha region.

The control laws were complex, incorporating the operation and coordination of no less than 19 different control surfaces on the HARV: six thrust-vectoring paddles, two ailerons, two rudders, two stabilators, two flaps, four leading-edge slats, and a speed brake. When moveable nose strakes were added to the vehicle in the third research phase, that number increased to 21.

In their work with the F-18 HARV, researchers were trying to validate control-law design methods for this new region even as they determined what sort of flying qualities would be acceptable to pilots operating aircraft at high angles of attack. Engineers first looked at the amount of control power the HARV might require based on various simulations, including simulated combat maneuvering in Langley's DMS facility, and designed control laws based on those results. These laws were then flown on the F-18 HARV to validate the design models and process and to gain pilot feedback on handling characteristics of the aircraft in actual flight.

In order to make the aircraft acceptable to pilots, the HARV control laws needed to give the aircraft predictable flight characteristics offering adequate

---

[25] Schneider, interviewed by Lane E. Wallace, 10 August 2001; Smolka, interviewed by Lane E. Wallace, 17 August 2001. The pilots improved with experience in the oddly balanced airplane: Schneider's last in-flight refueling took only 28 seconds to initiate. Most jet fighters have a relatively short range. Because landing to refuel takes time and fuel, Dryden research aircraft such as the F-18 and the F-15 refueled from airborne tankers from Edwards Air Force Base.

[26] Bowers, interviewed by Lane E. Wallace, 29 March 2001; Gilbert, interviewed by Lane E. Wallace, 13 August 2001.

[27] When a pilot moves the control stick it results in the movement of a control surface. Just how much that surface is moves, or how fast it moves, can be varied, and these are "gains."

maneuverability without making the plane too difficult to control. To help pilot feedback be more relevant to designers of future control laws and fighter aircraft, evaluation of each version of the control laws on the F-18 HARV included practice combat maneuvering with another aircraft. Pilot feedback was recorded using the "Cooper-Harper" rating system, in which pilots scored the difficulty of accomplishing maneuvers in the aircraft on a scale of 1 to 10. While this rating system is subjective as well as quantitative, it is widely used in research and in test flight and has proven an extremely valuable tool in evaluating aircraft handling characteristics and agility.[28]

In general, the control laws flown on the F-18 HARV worked well although some versions initially exhibited problems and the first set, designed by McDonnell Douglas and Honeywell and designated NASA-0, required more than a little of tweaking before they would work reliably. And when a Langley-designed control law called NASA-1 was first flown, an incorrect numerical value in the software caused a vibration in the airframe so noticeable that one pilot described the HARV on that flight as a "six-million-dollar vibrating chair." This particular control law also proved too sensitive and caused some pilot-induced oscillation problems before it was modified. In addition, there were differences among control-law performances between simulation and actual flight. These differences initially produced difficulties because there were slight time delays in how the aircraft sensors sampled information and processed them in the F-18's four flight computers. But the problems were quickly ironed out, and there were no major or unpleasant surprises in subsequent software versions.[29]

In addition to designing control laws and determining effective control-law design tools and methodology, HATP engineers also tried to develop useful guidelines for

the degree of control effectiveness a pilot really needed at high angles of attack. Of particular concern to both NASA and the U.S. Navy was determining guidelines for exactly how much longitudinal and lateral control power, or control effectiveness, would be required for a pilot to maintain control of an aircraft while maneuvering in high-alpha conditions. At high angles of attack many high-performance aircraft had encountered a phenomenon known as "alpha hang-up" in which the nose of the aircraft remained at a high angle of attack despite pilot inputs commanding full-down stabilator. Some designs had incorporated "alpha limiters" into the control system to prevent the aircraft from entering this potentially dangerous area. If aircraft were to have maximum maneuverability at high angles of attack, however, a better solution was required. The thrust-vectoring system on the F-18 HARV provided both the ability to reach the high angles of attack at which this problem occurred and a margin of safety in which to explore the phenomenon; the thrust-vectoring capability of the HARV meant it would have more than adequate control power to force the nose of the aircraft down.

Two sets of experiments were conducted to determine control power guidelines at high angles of attack. One, called High Alpha Nose-down Guidelines, or HANG, examined the amount of pitch control authority required to maintain control at high angles of attack. A companion experiment, the High Alpha Investigation of Requirements for Roll and Yaw, or HAIRRY, evaluated the amount of rolling and yawing moment necessary to safely execute a rolling maneuver at high angles of attack.

Both sets of experiments relied heavily on piloted simulations in which different gains, or levels of control effectiveness, were tried by a group of pilots, including several guest pilots from both the Navy and the Air Force. Some of the control guidelines generated by those simulations were then flown on the F-18 HARV to verify the simulator results in actual flight, including two flights flown by Navy test pilot Lt. Dave Prater in November 1992. The results of both the simulator and flight HANG and HAIRRY experiments generated extremely useful information for the military about the amount of control effectiveness that would be required for future fighter

[28] The Cooper-Harper rating system is a scale from one to ten by which research pilots can indicate their subjective judgment of the handling qualities of an airplane, 1 being the best. 1-3 means "meets desirable criteria (Level 1), 4-6 means "meets acceptable criteria," (Level 2), and 7-9 are "unacceptable" (Level 3). A rating of 10 represents loss of control. Schneider, interviewed by Lane E. Wallace, 24 August 1995; Schneider, interviewed by Lane E. Wallace, 10 August 2001; Gilbert, interviewed by Lane E. Wallace, 13 August 2001; John Foster, interviewed by Lane E. Wallace, 14 August 2001; Tom Bundick, interviewed by Lane E. Wallace, 14 August 2001; "Flight Test Plan: HARV NASA-1 Control Law Evaluation, draft, 1 October 1992, DFRC Historical Reference Collection; "F-18 Objectives and Requirements Specification Document F: Flight Control and Flying Qualities Study," 5 May 1987, NASA Dryden Flight Research Center Historical Reference Collection; Joe Pahle, interviewed by Lane E. Wallace, 16 August 2001.

[29] Bowers, interviewed by Lane E. Wallace, 29 March 2001; Schneider, interviewed by Lane E. Wallace, 10 August 2001; Bundick, interviewed by Lane E. Wallace, 14 August 2001; Pahle, interviewed by Lane E. Wallace, 16 August 2001.

aircraft designed to operate in this new region of high-alpha flight.[30]

Propulsion Research

Another goal of the HATP was to conduct research in the area of engine performance at high angles of attack. To this end, both HARV engines were fitted with real-time thrust measuring (RTTM) sensors to evaluate and quantify the F-18's engine performance, including the effects of inlet distortion during thrust-vectored and high-alpha flight. The RTTM system developed and flown on the HARV seemed to work well, with a discrepancy of less than 10 percent from thrust predictions. In addition to providing important information on engine thrust in dynamic conditions, the research helped develop a new tool for quantifying engine thrust.[31]

Concern existed about whether the aircraft engines would operate reliably with the low and highly distorted engine inlet airflows that occurred during thrust-vectoring at high-alpha or even operating an aircraft in high-alpha conditions. During earlier testing with an F-14 at Dryden, over 80 engine stalls had occurred at high angles of attack. In addition to gathering data on the engine's thrust, then, researchers also wanted to know more about the behavior of airflows within the engine inlet at high angles of attack.

One of the reasons the F-18 had been selected as the HARV aircraft was that its engine inlet design and General Electric F404-GE-400 engines had proven reliable at high angles of attack. Yet because even the F-18 could not sustain flight at extremely high angles of attack (above 55 degrees alpha), little was known about what would occur in terms of airflow or pressures within the engine inlet in those flight conditions. If future fighters were to make use of thrust-vectoring, or operate at extremely high angles of attack, designers needed more data on engine inlet dynamics in those conditions.

To collect some of that data, the F-18 HARV was modified with a 40-probe total pressure measurement rake installed immediately in front of the right engine compressor face, inside the engine inlet, as well as pressure-measuring instrumentation along the inlet. In addition to pressure ports, the rake also incorporated thermal and strain gage instrumentation; a dedicated instrumentation system recorded the copious data generated by the probe and instrumentation. The rake, designed by researchers at Dryden, Lewis, and General Electric, was both an innovative and inexpensive design. It featured a single-piece, wagon-wheel configuration that did not require major modification of the inlet and, perhaps even more important, was applicable to other engine and aircraft models. Once the aircraft had been modified with the new inlet rake, the propulsion research portion of the F-18 HARV Phase II flights began on 14 January 1994.

The goals of the HARV propulsion experiments were to evaluate the effect of rapid maneuvering on inlet distortion and engine stability during aircraft departures, and then compare the actual in-flight flow patterns with those predicted through CFD methods. Because the Lewis Research Center's contribution to the project focused on engine research, that center took the lead for this area of HATP research, although correlating wind tunnel experiments were simultaneously conducted at Langley, extensive CFD work was done at Ames as well as Lewis, and Dryden still managed and supervised the flight portion of the experiments.[32]

[30] Foster, interviewed by Lane E. Wallace, 14 August 2001; Bowers, interviewed by Lane E. Wallace, 29 March 2001; "F-18 High Alpha Research Vehicle Program Objectives and Requirements Document HH," 1 October 1992, DFRC Historical Reference Collection; "F-18 #840 HARV Flight Chronology," undated document, DFRC Historical Reference Collection; "Flight Test Plan: HARV NASA-1 Control Law Evaluation, draft, 1 October 1992, DFRC Historical Reference Collection; Pahle, interviewed by Lane E. Wallace, 16 August 2001.

[31] "F-18 HARV Real-Time Thrust Method (RTTM)," viewgraphs, from XRP 1994 Annual Report, Ron Ray, P.I., DFRC Historical Reference Collection; Ron Ray, interviewed by Lane E. Wallace, 17 August 2001; Memo from Robert W. Kempel to the Society of Flight Test Engineers, Inc., nominating the F-18 HARV project/team for the 1993 "Kelly" Johnson Achievement Award, 8 March 1993.

[32] Bowers, "F-18 High Alpha Research Vehicle: A 1995 Overview," draft, from Al Bowers personal files; "Extreme Attitude and Rate Inlet Flow Research," draft HATP document, 10 July 1987, DFRC Historical Reference Collection; "F-18 #840 HARV Flight Chronology," undated document, DFRC Historical Reference Collection; "High Alpha Research Vehicle Phase II Flight Test Plan," HA90-70-202, June 1990, DFRC Historical Reference Collection; "F-18 HARV Objectives and Requirements Document T: "High Alpha Thrust Degradation and Prediction Study," 27 August 1993 update, DFRC Historical Reference Collection; letter to Richard Burley, NASA Lewis Research Center regarding HARV Flight Inlet Data Program from William G. Steenken, Engine Operability and GEAE HARV Program manager, GE Aircraft Engines, 11 January 1993, DFRC Historical Reference Collection; Gilbert, interviewed by Lane E. Wallace, 13 August 2001; "F-18 HARV Objectives and Requirements Document XX: Propulsion Inlet Research," 20 April 1993, DFRC Historical Reference Collection; "F-18 HARV Propulsion Research, ARTS Review viewgraphs, 7 January 1993, DFRC Historical Reference Collection.

The F-18 HARV propulsion experiments produced some unexpected results. At high angles of attack the thrust generated by the engines was not as high as predicted–important information any future designers of thrust-vectoring-dependent aircraft would want to have. But at the same time, the F-18's engines proved surprisingly robust, even at extremely high angles of attack. The engine inlet rake allowed researchers to collect valuable data on airflow distortion at high angles of attack. Although the HARV pilots performed abrupt high-alpha maneuvers and intentional "departures" of the aircraft in an attempt to cause engine stalls for study purposes, the only engine stalls ever actually produced were "pop" stalls that were self-recovering.[33]

Phase II flights of the F-18 HARV concluded on 30 June 1994. Although the HATP research effort had originally called for only two research phases, interest in further research, especially in the area of advanced control concepts, prompted an extension of the program into a third phase.

The High Alpha Technology Program: Phase III

The initial concept for a third phase of the HATP was simply to take advantage of the F-18 HARV's unique high-alpha capabilities to "conduct selected flight experiments" in the high-alpha realm of flight.[34] In the end, these experiments focused primarily on exploring the use of forebody controls to enhance the aircraft's high-angle-of-attack controllability and

maneuverability. But the final HARV research phase also included some flight-validation experiments for a set of standard maneuvers designed to evaluate the flying qualities of future fighter designs, as well as some joint NASA-Navy investigations into wing rock and "falling leaf" phenomena that had plagued fleet F-18s and other high-performance fighter aircraft. The final research stage also featured a guest pilot program in which Navy, industry, and other NASA pilots were given the opportunity to evaluate the F-18's flying qualities and expanded-envelope capabilities.

Phase III: Aircraft Modifications

The primary modification made to the F-18 HARV for the third phase of flight experiments was the fabrication and installation of a new radome section that incorporated two retractable strakes. The concept of nose strakes and, indeed, of using forebody controls to increase controllability and maneuverability of fighter aircraft at high angles of attack sprang from the way fighter-aircraft design had been evolving since the 1950s.

New fighter aircraft typically had long nose shapes that gave stations at the nose of the aircraft an equal or greater "moment arm," or leverage potential, than had the vertical tails. In the case of the F-18, the moment arm from the forebody to the center of gravity was more than twice that from the center of gravity to the vertical tails. This meant that a small control input at the aircraft's forebody could have a much greater impact on the plane's movement than a larger control input with the aircraft's twin rudders. Researchers and pilots already had discovered that even small imperfections or distortions in the basic shape of fighter aircraft noses could cause significant differences in flight characteristics.[35]

Another factor that argued for the potential of

Inlet Data Program from William G. Steenken, Engine Operability and GEAE HARV Program manager, GE Aircraft Engines, 11 January 1993, DFRC Historical Reference Collection; Gilbert, interviewed by Lane E. Wallace, 13 August 2001; "F-18 HARV Objectives and Requirements Document XX: Propulsion Inlet Research," 20 April 1993, DFRC Historical Reference Collection; "F-18 HARV Propulsion Research, ARTS Review viewgraphs, 7 January 1993, DFRC Historical Reference Collection.

[33] Schnieder, interviewed by Lane E. Wallace, 10 August 2001; letter to Denis Bessette regarding significance of HARV propulsion research to industry from William G. Steenken, Engine Operability and GEAE HARV Program manager, 6 January 1994, DFRC Historical Reference Collection; Ron Ray, interviewed by Lane E. Wallace, 17 August 2001; Meyer, interviewed by Lane E. Wallace, 9 August 2001; Albion H. Bowers, et. al, "An Overview of the NASA F-18 High Alpha Research Vehicle," 28.

[34] "High Alpha Technology Program (HATP) Plan," program plan, 19 March 1990, DFRC Historical Reference Collection.

[35] In its most familiar example, a moment arm is a lever. For a given weight, the farther from the fulcrum the less force necessary to lift the weight. In an aircraft, the farther a force is located from the center of gravity (point of rotation) the less force necessary to produce control. Schnieder, interview, 24 August 1995; Meyer, interviewed by Lane E. Wallace, 9 August 2001; Dan Murri, interviewed by Lane E. Wallace, 14 August 2001.

In addition to thrust-vectoring vanes in the exhaust stream, NASA's F-18 HARV eventually had two strakes that could be opened and closed–dubbed ANSER, for Actuated Nose Strakes for Enhanced Rolling–installed in the nose. Four feet long and six inches wide, the strakes could be operated individually in flight and were designed to interact with the nose vortices to produce yaw control at high angles of attack. The strakes, outlined in paint and extending from the white nose cone, are retracted in this photo.

One strake is open as its use in flight would dictate.

forebody controls was that at high angles of attack much of the aircraft's tail effectiveness was reduced because the aircraft fuselage interfered with airflow over the tail section. The forebody area, by contrast, would remain in undisturbed flow even at high angles of attack.

The F-18 HARV was not the first aircraft to explore forebody control concepts. The Grumman X-29 research aircraft flown at Dryden in the 1980s and early 1990s had experimented with a pneumatic forebody control system that blew air out of ports in the sides of the aircraft forebody to enhance yaw control at high angles of attack. The X-29 system was rudimentary, however, in that it was not incorporated into the aircraft's flight control system. Researchers looked into developing the concept further for the F-18 HARV but concluded that the technology was not as mature as the actuated, retractable nose strakes concept developed at Langley. Consequently, the actuated nose strake

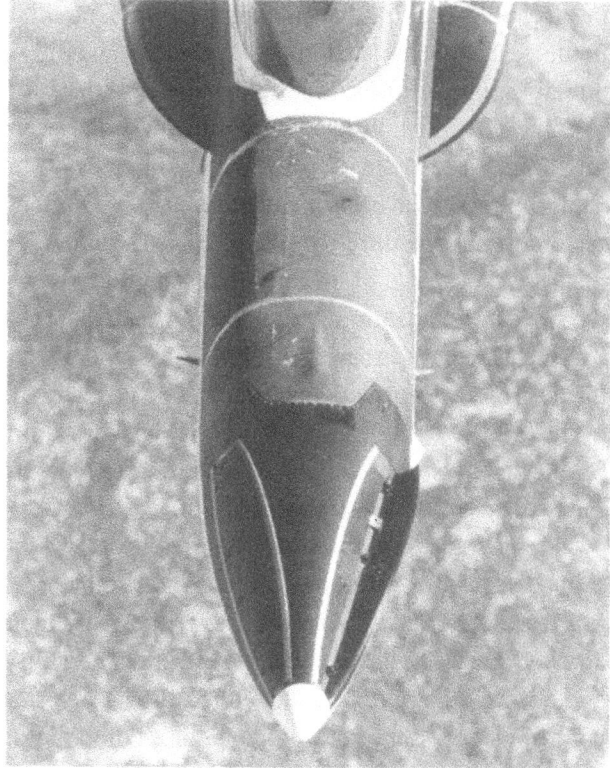

concept was selected for fabrication and installation on the F-18 HARV for flight experiments in forebody controls.[36]

To reduce the cost and complexity of the strake modification, Langley engineers designed the strakes to be incorporated into the radome nose section of the F-18. This allowed the team to simply fabricate a new radome section to replace the HARV's existing radome section (which did not have a radar unit in it). This modification would be impractical for a fleet F-18, because the modification would interfere with the radar component in the radome section of all combat F-18s. However, while only the radome strakes were tested in flight, Langley researchers also conducted wind tunnel tests with strakes placed further back on

[36] Fisher, et. al, "Effect of Actuated Forebody Strakes on the Forebody Aerodynamics of the NASA F-18 HARV, NASA Technical Memorandum 4774, October 1996, 1-3; Domingo A. Tavella, et. al, "Pneumatic Vortical Flow Control at High Angles of Attack," AIAA Paper 90-0098, presented at the 28th Aerospace Sciences Meeting (Reno, NV: 8–11 January 1990), 1-6; Daniel G. Murri, et. al, "Flight-Test Results of Actuated Forebody Strake Controls on the F-18 High alpha Research Vehicle, paper, presented at the High-Angle-of-Attack Technology Conference (NASA Langley Research Center, Hampton, VA: 17-19 September 1996), 2-7; Murri, interviewed by Lane E. Wallace, 14 August 2001.

the forebody, behind the radome section. The wind tunnel tests indicated that those strakes also would be effective control surfaces at high angles of attack.

The hydraulically operated aluminum strakes were positioned 120 degrees from the radome's bottom centerline and each had a planform area of 2.71 square feet, or about one third the size of an F-18 rudder. To measure the impact of the strakes on forebody flows, the strake modification also included the installation of 215 pressure ports around the radome, the strakes, and the nose cap, and an additional smoke port on each side of the radome to allow for better vortex visualization. Strain gages also were added to the radome to measure loads imposed by the strakes in flight.

At the same time, the F-18 HARV control laws and flight control system required modification to incorporate use of the strakes. Software used in the experiment allowed each strake to be deployed independently, and allowed the pilot to select either thrust-vectoring control alone, strake control alone, or a combination of both types of control inputs.

The nose strakes and radome section were developed, fabricated, and tested at Langley, and the first HARV flight with the nose-actuated strakes took place on 15 March 1995.[37]

Both strakes are open as the ground crew works on the aircraft.

Phase III: Experiments

The Actuated Nose Strakes for Enhanced Rolling (ANSER) flight experiments constituted the largest portion of the HATP Phase III effort. The experiments had three major objectives: to evaluate and document aerodynamic characteristics of the strakes and their impact on off-surface flows, and correlate those measurements with wind tunnel and CFD predictions; to document any enhancements in agility produced by the strakes and determine potential handling quality standards for high-angle-of-attack rolling maneuvers; and to validate the control-law design process used to integrate the strakes into the F-18's flight control system. To accomplish these objectives, the F-18 HARV used both open-loop and closed-loop (pilot-controlled) maneuvers. Comparison maneuvers were flown using strakes only, thrust-vectoring only, and a combination of the two.[38]

Some of the research results were surprising. As anticipated, the nose strakes became more effective at higher angles of attack, and when combined, the strakes and thrust-vectoring yielded more yaw control power than did either one individually. At angles of attack smaller than about 20 degrees, the strakes had little impact because they required some cross-flow on the aircraft forebody, a condition that occurred only at higher angles of attack. At flight conditions above about 25 degrees alpha, however, the strakes proved equally as effective as the thrust-vectoring controls. And at about 50 degrees alpha, the strakes had almost twice the yaw control power than the aircraft rudders provided at low angles of attack, even though the strakes were only one-third the size of the aircraft rudders.

[38] A *closed loop* system employs sensors which interpret the pilot's command and, through feedback, modify the original control input before it ever reaches the surface to be commanded. This is to ensure that the pilot does not over-control or damage the aircraft. An *open loop* control system has no feed back. Instead, there is a direct link between the pilot and the control systems, without any electronic interpretation.

[37] Bowers, et. al, "An Overview of the NASA F-18 High Alpha Research Vehicle," 28-30; Murri, interviewed by Lane E. Wallace, 14 August 2001; Dan Murri, email document to Lane Wallace regarding strake fabrication , 19 September 2001; Murri, et. al, "Flight-Test Results of Actuated Forebody Strake Controls on the F-18 High alpha Research Vehicle, 5-7; "F-18 #840 HARV Flight Chronology."

A few discrepancies existed between the flight test results and the wind and water tunnel predictions. For one, the vortex generated by the strakes proved to follow a higher trajectory on the actual aircraft than water tunnel tests had predicted. But the strakes also were about 15 percent less effective at high angles of attack than wind tunnel tests had indicated. Researchers ascribed this to notches cut out of the flight-worthy strake surfaces to enable them to fully retract to the conformal shape of the radome without interfering with the aircraft bulkhead in that section.

Yet the F-18 HARV ANSER flight experiments clearly illustrated the potential of forebody controls for enhancing yaw and rolling controllability and maneuverability at high angles of attack. In addition, the experiments helped to verify and refine ground predictions and design methods for forebody control systems. That information may prove important to future aircraft designers because forebody controls offer a potential solution to at least part of the problem inherent in a thrust-vectoring-dependent aircraft design. Thrust-vectoring derives its effectiveness from aircraft engines. If the engines were to fail, or if, in maneuvering the aircraft, the pilot pulled back on the throttle, the thrust-vectoring controls would lose much of their effectiveness. Forebody controls provide another control system option, or a back-up control system, at least for angles of attack above 20 degrees.[39]

Navy Evaluations/
STEMS

The F-18 HARV flight experiments were of particular interest to U.S. Navy officials for several reasons. First, data collected on the F-18 would be especially useful in naval applications because of the widespread use of F-18s in the fleet. And second, naval researchers also were trying to identify maneuvering requirements and corresponding design criteria for advanced fighters. Aircraft designs always involved trade-offs among various features, and naval researchers were interested in identifying the amount of control force required in order for a design to perform well at high angles of attack. The thrust-vectoring capability and instrumentation of the HARV offered a unique opportunity to explore these areas in flight and collect valuable data to verify the predictions of wind tunnel and computational studies.

In 1992, as part of Phase II of the HATP, a Navy test pilot flew the HARV to help validate simulation methods and results in a joint study on longitudinal control forces and handling characteristics of the F-18 being conducted by the Navy and Langley. The results proved very helpful, so additional Navy evaluation flight experiments were incorporated into Phase III of the HATP to allow Navy researchers to collect data on lateral-directional control phenomena and handling characteristics to correlate with their ground research studies. In particular, Navy researchers were interested in investigating both the "wing rock" phenomenon, in which F-18 wings would oscillate at high angles of attack, and the "falling leaf" phenomenon, where uncommanded oscillations in roll and yaw could cause an aircraft to "fall" out of the sky in a fashion similar to that of a falling leaf.

In both cases, the thrust-vectoring and spin chute present on the F-18 HARV gave researchers the security of knowing they could explore these potentially dangerous phenomena without high risk to the aircraft or crew. In both sets of Navy evaluations, the thrust-vectoring system of the HARV also allowed

[39] Murri, interviewed by Lane E. Wallace, 14 August 2001; "High Alpha Research Vehicle Phase 3 Flight Test Plan," HA94-2-03, February 1995, 6-10; Murri, et. al, "Flight-Test Results of Actuated Forebody Strake Controls on the F-18 High alpha Research Vehicle, p.2-10, 18-19; Bowers, et. al, "An Overview of the NASA F-18 High Alpha Research Vehicle," 28-30; David Fisher, et. al, "Effect of Actuated Forebody Strakes on the Forebody Aerodynamics of the NASA F-18 HARV, NASA Technical Memorandum 4774, October 1996, 1-3, 28; Schneider, interviewed by Lane E. Wallace, 24 August 1995; Gilbert, interviewed by Lane E. Wallace, 13 August 2001.

[40] J. Lackey and Lt. D. Prater, USN, "Limited Navy Flying Qualities and Performance Evaluation of the NASA F-18 HARV," Technical Memorandum TM-93-11 SA. 21 June 1993, i, DFRC Historical Reference Collection; "Project Test Plan #1573," Naval Air Warfare Center Aircraft Division Flight Test and Engineering Group unclassified document, 7 March 1994, DFRC Historical Reference Collection; Guy Norris, "NASA will use its HARV F-18 to tackle 'falling leaf' problem," *Flight International*, 19-25 June 1996, 22; "High Alpha Research Vehicle Phase 3 Flight Test Plan," HA94-2-03, February 1995, 10, 14; David Williams, et. al, "Comparison of Flight and Sub-scale Model Wing Rock Characteristics of an F-18 Aircraft," Final Report for NASA Grant NCA2-513, University of Notre Dame, 30 April 1993, ii, 1-2, DFRC Historical Reference Collection.

pilots, in simulated combat maneuvers, to perform direct comparisons in maneuvering effectiveness of the aircraft with and without thrust-vectoring.[40]

Phase III of the F-18 HARV flights also included experiments aimed at flight-validating a set of standard maneuvers that had been proposed to evaluate the flying qualities of future fighter designs. The Standard Evaluation Maneuver Set (STEMS) experiments sought to establish performance standards for various maneuvers; prior to the STEM experiments, aircraft performance was evaluated merely on the basis of a quantified aircraft response.[41]

These two photos illustrate the deflection angles possible on the NASA F-18 HARV, dubbed "Silk Purse." With the jet firmly anchored, one engine is operated in afterburner. The paddles can clearly be seen vectoring the exhaust that, in flight, would afford more radical maneuvering by the jet.

Conclusion

The Phase III flight experiments and the HATP officially ended with the 383rd flight of the F-18 HARV on 29 May 1996–a flight that pilot Ed Schneider concluded with a low-level fly-by over Dryden. The crew then took the aircraft to various Air Force bases, to McDonnell Douglas facilities in St. Louis, Missouri, and to Langley during the following six months, but actual flight research with the F-18 HARV ended in May.[42]

The HATP was initially envisioned as a five-year program. It lasted 12 years, and was not only an extremely productive and successful flight research effort, but also a remarkable inter-center NASA research program, successfully joining the efforts of multiple disciplines and researchers at four NASA centers. As NASA field centers have a long tradition of independence and competition, this alone was a major feat.

But the HATP also accomplished two other significant goals. First, the project offered researchers and designers inside and outside of NASA an exceptional testbed for investigating many aspects of high-alpha flight, a region of the flight envelope not well understood. The program produced a wide variety of detailed, quantitative, and flight-validated data in aerodynamics, propulsion, controls, and handling qualities in this new and complex realm of flight.

Second, by planning and coordinating the project among four NASA centers, the HATP integrated research in CFD, simulation, wind tunnels, and flight. This enabled researchers at all levels to gain valuable correlating data from other methods investigating the same area–whether in aerodynamic phenomena and flows, controls, propulsion, or handling characteristics. In addition to verifying and refining mathematical models, simulations, ground methods, and tools, this close coordination allowed HATP researchers to correct and refine their methods and tools as they progressed, making the HATP and the F-18 HARV research more accurate and productive.

Another important aspect of the program was the inclusion of pilots, researchers, engineers, and managers from outside agencies throughout the course of the research, helping not only to disseminate data and developments that resulted from the HATP research but also providing an opportunity for both military and civilian representatives to give the HATP team input on additional data that might be of interest to them. In this way, the HATP effort was able to sustain relevance to those who would be the eventual users of the technology. In addition to the two Navy evaluations and the guest-pilot program, the HATP team sponsored several high-alpha symposia as well as several workshops focused on more specific research areas. The NASA team also conducted a 1993 industry/Department of Defense "tour" of the HATP and F-18 HARV program that provided participants with a valuable opportunity to exchange information among all who were investigating the high-alpha realm of flight.[43]

Although the F-18 HARV was the first aircraft used to successfully demonstrate multi-axis thrust-vectoring in flight, proving this possible was not the real goal of the program. The two goals of the HATP were to develop the necessary technology–such as control laws and systems as well as pilot displays–for a thrust-vectored aircraft, and to use the rudimentary F-18 HARV thrust-vectoring system to achieve and sustain high-alpha flight, enabling researchers to explore the dynamics and phenomena that existed there. The HATP provided valuable results in both of these areas.

In addition, the F-18 HARV program inspired or pioneered the development and maturation of numerous technologies and systems, including the smoke-generating and PGME dye systems used to help researchers visualize separated airflows, the rotating LEX pressure rake, the single-piece engine inlet rake, the actuated forebody strakes, a flush air-data system and, of course, and the flight control laws and systems necessary to integrate both thrust-vectoring and nose strakes into the F-18's flight control system.

Because the flush air-data system eliminated the

---

[41] Bowers, "F-18 High Alpha Research Vehicle: A 1995 Overview"; "High Alpha Research Vehicle Phase 3 Flight Test Plan," HA94-2-03, February 1995, 13-14.

[42] "F-18 #840 HARV Flight Chronology."

[43] "NASA High Alpha Technology Program: Overview/Status/Plans/Deliverables," viewgraphs of presentation for HATP Industry/DOD Tour, May-June 1993, DFRC Historical Reference Collection; Luat T. Nguyen, "Summary of 1993 HATP Industry/DOD Tour," viewgraphs, 8 July 1993, DFRC Historical Reference Collection; memo to HARV Project leads from Victoria Regenie regarding notes from participants of the industry tour, undated, DFRC Historical Reference Collection.

need for a protruding pitot tube, it had great appeal to designers of future hypersonic and space vehicles and fighter aircraft. The hypersonic and space vehicle designers, such as those working on the X-33 reusable launch vehicle and the High Speed Civil Transport, liked the idea of a flush air-data system because of the difficulty of protecting a protruding pitot tube from the extreme heat generated by hypersonic flight and re-entry, while military aircraft designers were interested because of its low-observability potential. A flush air-data system will undoubtedly find its way into other applications regardless of how extensively thrust-vectoring is incorporated into future designs.

Data generated by the F-18 HARV and the HATP also allowed researchers to validate and refine ground models, methods, and tools for predicting the behavior of high-performance aircraft at high angles of attack. Researchers now know, for example, how big an impact even small amounts of surface roughness can have on the aerodynamics of an aircraft at high angles of attack, and have adjusted their wind tunnel and computational predictions accordingly. Beyond creating better research and design tools and methods, this data gave manufacturers greater confidence in these ground methods and tools for predicting aircraft behavior in the complex realm of high-alpha flight. Future fighters, for example, may not experience the wing rock and tail buffet problems encountered by the F-18 after it entered service. The F-18 HARV flights also provided valuable information to the military and industry about the amount of control needed to keep an aircraft controllable and maneuverable at high angles of attack, which will help maximize design efficiency and eliminate problems such as alpha hang-up in future fighter aircraft.

The F-18 HARV and the HATP research effort significantly expanded knowledge and understanding of a new and complex realm of flight while helping to develop new technology and systems for high-alpha flight. It was a challenging effort, requiring cooperation and coordination among different engineering disciplines, outside agencies, and NASA centers throughout more than a decade. But many of the NASA researchers who were involved in the F-18 HARV and HATP today consider it among the strongest programs in their experience, and one of their proudest career achievements.[44]

---

[44] Meyer, interviewed by Lane E. Wallace, 9 August 2001; Gatlin, interviewed by Lane E. Wallace, 14 August 2001; Pahle, interviewed by Lane E. Wallace, 16 August 2001; Schneider, interviewed by Lane E. Wallace, 10 August 2001; Bessette, interviewed by Lane E. Wallace, 10 August 2001; Gilbert, interviewed by Lane E. Wallace, 13 August 2001; Bowers, interviewed by Lane E. Wallace, 29 March 2001; Chambers, interviewed by Lane E. Wallace, 15 August 2001; Dave Fisher, Dan Banks, Robert Hall, Joseph Chambers, Jim Luckring and Dan Murri, email document to Lane Wallace regarding results and lessons of the F-18 HARV program, 18 September 2001.

Chapter Three
The X-31

In contrast to the F-18 HARV, which was developed primarily to help researchers better understand the aerodynamics and phenomena occurring in the high-alpha realm of flight, the X-31 was developed to prove the practical utility of a fighter that could operate in the post-stall (PST), or high-alpha, region. The X-31 program had four goals: to quickly provide a demonstration of high-agility maneuvering concepts, to investigate the tactical benefits of Enhanced Fighter Maneuverability (EFM) technologies, to validate a low-cost international prototyping concept, and to develop the design requirements and database to support future applications.[1]

Accomplishing these goals required a team of government and industry partners whose coordination was complicated by the geographic and linguistic barriers of one ocean and two languages. The X-31 represented the first international X-Plane project, combining research efforts of Rockwell International and the German aerospace company Messerschmitt-Bölkow-Blohm on opposite sides of the Atlantic throughout the 1970s and early 1980s. It achieved goals that neither country could have reached alone, yet managerial and organizational challenges of the program presented perhaps greater obstacles than the technical ones. The program succeeded as much because of the innovative and dedicated efforts of its managers as it did because of the technical expertise of team members.

The seeds of the X-31 program were planted on both sides of the Atlantic in the early 1970s. The U.S. military and, consequently, the U.S. aerospace industry, had become concerned with increased maneuverability and safety at high angles of attack because of the unacceptably high rate of aircraft losses in the Vietnam War era. That harsh historical impetus did not drive the Germans' search for improved maneuverability; theirs was a motivation perhaps even more pressing. With East Germany and other Eastern Block countries bordering West German territory, German military and aircraft designers knew that if hostilities broke out, their fighters would be in close-in combat almost from the moment of takeoff. The Americans' pre-Vietnam strategy of building high-speed fighters that relied on beyond visual range (BVR) engagements using stand-off missile launches was an approach the Germans would not have the luxury of employing.

In the early 1970s, MBB had begun the design process for what would eventually become the Eurofighter. New short-range and intermediate-range missiles were being developed that could lock onto a fighter's frontal aspect as well as its engine exhaust, introducing the additional tactical advantages of an aircraft that could make extremely sharp turns to point at an adversary. At the same time, an MBB engineer, Wolfgang Herbst, began arguing that the best way to gain tactical advantage in close-in combat would be with an aircraft that could perform well in the post-stall region of flight–up to 70 degrees angle of attack–where traditional aerodynamic controls became ineffective. Herbst asserted that an aircraft capable of maneuvering well at extremely high angles of attack could turn more quickly in close quarters and therefore gain an important advantage over opponents.

He conducted the first digital simulations of air combat involving post-stall flight in 1974. The simulations were predicated on the use of thrust-vectoring to achieve post-stall maneuverability. These digital simulations were followed by manned simulations in the IABG facility at Ottobrun, Germany, in 1977. In the manned simulations, two identical aircraft were pitted against each other, the only difference being that one was limited to 30 degrees alpha and the other could maneuver at angles of attack up to 70 degrees. The results were impressive, but resistance to the idea of maneuvering in the post-stall arena remained strong within the German aerospace community. There was concern about the accuracy of aerodynamic predictions used to create the simulations since high-alpha aerodynamics were complex and not well understood. There also were concerns about pilot disorientation at high angles of attack, as well as some disagreement as to whether PST maneuvers would give a pilot any tactical advantage; some argued that post-stall maneuvering would render a fighter so slow that it would be a sitting duck for follow-on attacks. Others also argued that while the simulation results had been impressive,

[1]"X-31 Enhanced Fighter Maneuverability Program Final Report, Volume 1," videotape record, from Michael Francis personal files.

they had been demonstrated only in "one-versus-one" engagements, whereas most actual combat engagements were "one-versus-many" situations.

Herbst responded with another piloted simulation at McDonnell Douglas in St. Louis, Missouri, where he and several other MBB engineers had worked in the late 1960s. McDonnell Douglas had a dome simulation facility that could link three pilots, enabling a thrust-vectored aircraft to be pitted against two opponents. The simulations at McDonnell Douglas took place in 1978 and the results were, again, impressive. Yet doubts about the possibilities and true tactical benefits of the concept lingered, so Herbst began lobbying for design and building of a technical demonstrator aircraft to test and prove the concept in flight. MBB could not afford the cost of such a program on its own, however, and Herbst was unable to find another European aerospace company interested in working on a demonstrator program with MBB.[2]

Meanwhile, engineers at Rockwell International also were looking for ways to increase the maneuverability of fighter aircraft. Since the early 1970s, Rockwell's California contingent had worked with the U.S. Air Force and NASA's Dryden Flight Research Center on the Highly Maneuverable Aircraft Technology (Hi-MAT) testbed–a remotely piloted, jet-powered scale model built to explore design concepts and technology that could increase the maneuverability of fighter aircraft. In the early 1980s, engineers at Rockwell's Columbus, Ohio, installation also were working with the U.S. Navy on its initial single-vane thrust-vectoring research with an F-14 Tomcat fighter.

As the 1970s came to a close, researchers at Rockwell also had a significant motivation for expanding the company's horizons and finding new partnerships. Cancellation of the B-1 program, resulting in the layoff of nearly 25,000 employees, had taken a toll on the company's workload, its workforce, and morale. Rockwell's management quickly decided the company needed to expand its base beyond being a one-program house. And since there were few new aircraft programs to pursue within the U.S., Rockwell was actively seeking international partnerships and new aircraft development projects.

This led Rockwell to support the SAAB JAS-39 Gripen development program–a Swedish program in which MBB also was involved. It was at SAAB, and also at international American Institute of Aeronautics and Astronautics (AIAA) meetings, where Rockwell's Mike Robinson and MBB's Herbst met. And when Herbst began talking to Robinson about developing a demonstrator aircraft for the post-stall maneuvering concept, he found Robinson and Rockwell very receptive to the idea of a possible joint venture.[3]

Throughout 1982, Robinson and Herbst compiled a briefing that they presented on 11 February 1983 to Jim Allburn, the Tactical Technology Office chief at the Defense Advanced Research Projects Agency (DARPA). The proposal suggested a multi-phase research effort, including design and testing of an actual aircraft, to demonstrate the tactical benefits of post-stall maneuvering. Robinson and Herbst dubbed their proposal the Super Normal Attitude Kinetic Enhancement (SNAKE) program. Allburn approved funds for an initial study of the concept, which Rockwell and MBB pursued throughout 1984-1985. The results, presented to DARPA and the German Ministry of Defense in December 1985, reinforced Herbst's contention that the super-maneuverability concept had promise. The report also concluded that if an aircraft demonstrator were to be developed to test the concept further in flight, it should be a custom-built, dedicated research aircraft.[4]

Rockwell and MBB had considered numerous options for a research vehicle, including modifying an F-15C, an F-16A, an F-18, and an X-29A. They even considered modifying a North American (then Rockwell) F-86 Sabre with thrust-vectoring capability. But the two companies finally concluded that the costs of retrofitting and modifying an existing aircraft were higher than simply starting with a clean sheet and designing and building a demonstrator aircraft from scratch. And building an entirely new aircraft

[2] Hannes Ross, interviewed by the author, 18 February 2002; "X-31 Questions," Hannes Ross email to Lane Wallace, 17 February 2002; "Roll-Out," MBB Document, 1 March 1990, DFRC Historical Reference Collection, 4-6.

[3] Michael Robinson, interviewed by the author, 15 February 2002 and 27 March 2002; Ross, interviewed by the author, 18 February 2002; Col. Michael Francis, USAF (Ret.), interviewed by author Burlingame, CA, 14 February 2002; "Roll-Out," 12; "X-31 Questions," Hannes Ross email to Lane Wallace, 17 February 2002.

[4] "Roll-Out," 12-15; Col. Michael Francis, interview, 14 February 2002; "X-31 Enhanced Fighter Maneuverability Program Final Report, Volume 1," videotape recording.

also would allow them to maximize the design's application for their research work.[5]

By fortuitous coincidence, the U.S. Congress passed the Nunn-Quayle amendment in 1986 to encourage international research and development efforts. The legislation provided both the funds and the legislative umbrella for a full-scale international research aircraft program. John Retelle, DARPA program manager for the SNAKE project, immediately scrambled to acquire Nunn-Quayle funds and the approval to develop and build the dedicated research aircraft his organization had proposed. In May 1986, a Memorandum of Agreement (MOA) was signed for a joint German-American research effort designated the Enhanced Fighter Maneuverability program that would result in the design, construction, and flight test of the X-31. The program's ambitious goal was to have the research aircraft flying by 1989.

In August 1986, DARPA designated the U.S. Navy as its managing agent for the program. Although DARPA first approached the Air Force, priorities had begun to shift again in the Air Force with the development of the Advanced Tactical Fighter (ATF). The SNAKE concept of close-in, slow-speed maneuverability ran counter to the prevailing Air Force interest in using stealth, high speed, and BVR missile capabilities to protect its fighters, and the X-31 program no longer fit Air Force objectives. On the German side, the Bundsamt fur Wehrtechnik und Beschaffung (BWB) managed the program for the German Ministry of Defense.[6]

Setting up an international flight research program was a difficult challenge in many respects, and there was no blueprint for how to design or manage it well. But given the sensitivities inherent in an international industry/government cooperative research and development program, the X-31 program structure worked exceptionally well. Under the MOA, Rockwell was given overall program management responsibility, with MBB as an associate contractor. To resolve management issues, it was also agreed that Rockwell

engineers working at MBB's Munich facility would take day-to-day direction from MBB management, and MBB engineers at Rockwell would operate in a reciprocal manner.

In addition, the MOA stipulated that the partners clearly define and separate work packages and responsibilities as part of the project's design-study phase. Part of that division of labor was decided on the basis of funds available for the work; the MOA also specified that no transfer of money would take place between the two countries or companies, except in special instances. The German government provided funds for MBB's work, the U.S. government for Rockwell's. The funding was not evenly divided, but neither were the intellectual contributions of the two partners. The U.S. provided approximately 80 percent of the program funding, but the Germans brought to the table far more knowledge about post-stall phenomena, maneuvers, and tactical possibilities. As one of the DARPA X-31 program managers described it, "We did things we knew how to do. The Germans did things that had never been done."[7]

The initial goal of the "phase II" contract awarded to Rockwell and MBB in September 1986 was to perform design studies for a demonstrator aircraft, but the two companies had actually begun work on potential designs even before the MOA was signed. In the first phase of the study, Rockwell and MBB had worked together on research and development of two different designs. One possibility proposed by Rockwell bore some hereditary resemblance to the HiMAT vehicle. Tests in the NASA Langley Research Center's 30-by-60-foot wind tunnel indicated that the initial configuration had unacceptable stability and control characteristics, but a modified design showed promise. MBB, meanwhile, favored a derivative of an advanced canard fighter known as the TKF-90, a predecessor to the European Fighter Aircraft, or Eurofighter.[8]

Both companies realized that if they were to get approval and funding to build an aircraft, the design

[5] Robinson, interviewed by the author, 15 February 2002 and 27 March 2002.

[6] "X-31 Enhanced Fighter Maneuverability Program Final Report, Volume 1," videotape record; "Roll-Out," 12-21; "The X-31: The First International US/German Experimental Program," Deutsche Aerospace viewgraphs, DFRC Historical Reference Collection; "X-31: Post Stall Pioneer +," viewgraphs, from presentation by Col. Michael Francis, USAF (Ret).

[7] Francis, interviewed by author, 14 February 2002; Robinson, interviewed by the author, 27 March 2002; Harvey Schellenger, interviewed by the author, 5 February 2002.

[8] "Roll-Out," 6-13; Partners in Freedom, 216-219; Michael Robinson, interviewed by the author, 27 March 2002; Harvey Schellenger, interviewed by the author, 5 February 2002; "Questions," Joseph R. Chambers email to Lane Wallace, 9 March 2002, Lane Wallace personal files.

The X-31, a joint German-American project, employed an original airframe. Two aircraft were built and flown. Visible in the head-on view of the X-31 are several distinguishing features of the aircraft, among them the fore planes, or canards, and the strakes on the aft fuselage. Apparent is the absence of any horizontal stabilizer. The canards and the thrust-vectoring paddles compensated for this absence in addition to providing high degrees of maneuverability.

they chose would need to be extremely cost-effective. Indeed, one of the four main goals articulated for the X-31 program was to validate a low-cost international prototyping concept. As a result, while the final configuration of the X-31 was a custom-built, one-off design, it drew heavily on existing components and design concepts.

Rockwell and MBB finally merged their design concepts into a single-tail, delta wing/canard design powered by a single General Electric F404 afterburning engine. On 23 February 1987, the design received its official "X-Plane" designation as the X-31A.[9] MBB was given responsibility for developing control laws for the flight control system and manufacturing both

the wings and the thrust-vectoring vanes. Rockwell was responsible for manufacturing the fuselage, canard, and vertical tail, and integrating the remaining systems and components. Assembly and initial flight tests of the aircraft would take place at Rockwell's Palmdale, California, facility.

As with the F-18 HARV, a low-cost method of vectoring thrust was needed for the X-31, and at that time

[9] There is sometimes confusion about the aircraft's designation as the "X-31" or the "X-31A." The "A" designation apparently derived from the tradition of designating an operational version of a design as an "A" model. In any event, the X-31A designation did not denote a change from an original "X-31" design. For simplification purposes, I refer to the aircraft as the "X-31" throughout this text.

the most workable low-cost thrust-vectoring concept was the external paddle system tested in the U.S. Navy F-14 flight test program. Although the paddle approach was chosen for the thrust-vectoring systems of both the X-31 and the F-18 HARV, the X-31's paddles were not made of the heavy Inconel steel used on the F-18 HARV. In addition to validating a low-cost prototyping approach, the X-31 team wanted the performance of the research aircraft to be similar enough to that of a modern fighter that the military would take the resulting flight-test data seriously. In the eyes of team members, that meant the X-31 had to be capable of supersonic flight. It also had to have a thrust-to-weight ratio of at least 1.0 in order to possess the performance and maneuverability characteristics the team hoped to demonstrate. The 2,000 pounds of extra weight the HARV paddle system added to the F-18 was simply too much, so MBB elected to build the X-31 paddles out of carbon-carbon composite. The material had been tested in high-temperature, electro-iron melting and used in space applications, but carbon composites were very brittle and the approach was considered much riskier than using Inconel. In the end, however, the weight-saving carbon paddles were manufactured, installed, and operated without penalties.[10]

Several other unique design elements were incorporated in the X-31. Its canard was designed more to improve the aerodynamic handling of the aircraft at high angles of attack than to generate additional lift. As the aircraft increased its angle of attack, the canard would angle down into the air stream to a maximum negative deflection of 55 degrees, helping to maintain some aerodynamic control even when the control surfaces at the trailing edge of the delta wing ceased to be effective. The X-31 also incorporated a belly-mounted inlet with an articulating lower lip that helped keep air flowing into the engine even at high angles of attack.[11]

Several other decisions regarding the design and fabrication of the X-31 were made primarily in the interest of keeping costs down. To keep the design simple, especially since the wings and fuselage were to be manufactured in separate locations, all the fuel was to be carried in a single fuselage tank. The aircraft also was designed to use "fly-away tooling." Tooling is used to keep components of an aircraft in place while the aircraft is assembled. This tooling is usually temporary and is separate from the aircraft fuselage.

In the case of the X-31, however, the fuselage bulkheads were designed to be strong enough to serve as the tooling. As a result, the company didn't have to build time-consuming and expensive tooling for the fuselage.

In another cost-saving effort, the X-31 also incorporated many off-the-shelf parts, although this had mixed results. The entire cockpit, canopy, and instrumentation suite were taken from an F-18. The landing gear and fuel pump came from an F-16, the flight control computers were modified versions of those used in the Air Force's C-130 High Technology Test Bed (HTTB) aircraft, the actuators were from a V-22, and the wheels and brakes came off a Cessna Citation jet. Off-the-shelf parts, however, often don't work adequately in secondary applications, and this created problems with the X-31. The actuators, for example, performed so poorly that the team wound up discarding them and designing new ones. The original generator, chosen because it was less expensive, was found to be incompatible with the X-31's environment and ended up having to be replaced with a more expensive model after all.

Initially, the team hoped to build three X-31 aircraft, but budgetary pressures made that impossible. In fact, there was some discussion–and budgetary pressure–to build only one model of the aircraft. In the end, researchers settled on building two, both to give them a back-up model if something went wrong with one aircraft and to increase the potential frequency of test flights. The team also wanted to fly the identical aircraft in combat scenarios against one another, with only one using its thrust-vectoring capability, to evaluate the difference made by thrust-vectoring. That never happened, but a second X-31 was extremely important to the program all the same–not only for scheduling and redundancy, but also because the aircraft had to do double duty as both flight- and ground-test vehicles.

At the program's outset, the decision was made not to build an Iron Bird that could be used to test components and software in the development process. Instead, the actual X-31 itself became an Iron Bird. When flight control engineers needed to test software

---

[10] Ross, interviewed by the author, 18 February 2002; Peter Huber, interviewed by the author, 7 February 2002; "Roll-Out," 6-11.

[11] "Roll-Out," 6-11; Francis, interviewed by author, 14 February 2002.

or components, they would bring their simulation benches from plants in El Segundo or Downey, California, to Rockwell's Palmdale facility and connect their computers to the X-31 sitting in the hangar. This eliminated the need to build a third airframe, but it also created a bottleneck and extensive delays in the manufacturing process as software engineers and manufacturing technicians fought for access to the aircraft.[12]

Construction of the X-31 began in 1987. Col. Tack Nix, then the X-31 program manager for DARPA, had previously managed several "black" programs, and he brought a philosophy of small, independent, co-located design and manufacturing teams to the X-31 program. MBB and Rockwell engineers were co-located in small areas within Rockwell, and some of Rockwell's engineers moved to Munich to help with the MBB work. There was a great deal of team-building required among those assigned to the program, a process that would be repeated when the program later moved to NASA, but once a certain level of trust had been established, work proceeded fairly smoothly.

Perhaps the toughest cross-cultural technical problem to be resolved in the manufacturing process involved the development of the X-31 control laws. The Germans had a very different approach to control-law development that used mathematical predictive models of the aircraft's behavior to program appropriate control responses to different commands and conditions. The Americans were accustomed to a more reactive type of control law, designed to read an aircraft's actual behavior and respond accordingly. The Rockwell engineers were initially skeptical about MBB's approach but, for proprietary reasons, MBB didn't want to divulge the secrets of its control-law techniques. Some friction arose over this, but eventually, as team trust grew, the control laws proved themselves in simulation. As Rockwell engineers became familiar with the German control laws, the laws became more trusted and accepted.[13]

Other concerns arose as a result of the team's international nature, such as how to allow MBB engineers to work at Rockwell's Palmdale plant without compromising the security of other classified and sensitive projects. Fortunately, the X-31 managers' practice of co-locating small teams in a common area made it easier for the international engineers to work together without having to wander through sensitive areas in each others' facilities. Program managers had also worried that the time difference between Rockwell's California facilities and MBB's Munich location would be a problem, but it ultimately worked to the team's advantage, giving the program a kind of virtual second shift. Unresolved problems could be transmitted from California to Germany or vice versa at the end of each workday. The engineers across the globe could then address the problems overnight and have solutions or ideas waiting for their colleagues upon their arrival at work the next morning. And once the start-up issues between the two locations were smoothed out, program managers found that the international partnership had another unexpected benefit as well. One of the most significant and ongoing problems faced in the X-31 program was the uncertainty of its funding. But the international nature of the X-31 program meant that neither country could cancel the program's funding without international repercussions, affording the program critical leverage and financial stability.[14]

While design and fabrication of the full-scale aircraft was underway in Munich and California, testing of scale models and components was being conducted at both Langley and the U.S. Navy's Patuxent River facility. Ground tests of the thrust deflector system were conducted at Patuxent River, and various wind tunnel and other tests were carried out at Langley. Drop tests of a scale model of the X-31 from a helicopter at Langley, for example, were conducted to investigate the vehicle's "out-of control" characteristics. The dynamically faithful model tests were done because computer simulations would simply freeze when the aircraft went too far out of control. Researchers wanted to know what to expect if the aircraft departed controlled flight at an extremely high angle of attack. Tests indicated that the aircraft's response in a departure situation would be much more violent

---

[12] John Sheen, interviewed by the author, 11 March 2002.

[13] Ross, interviewed by the author, 18 February 2002; Francis, interview, 14 February 2002; "X-31 Questions," Hannes Ross email to Lane Wallace, 17 February 2002; Rogers Smith, interviewed by the author, 16 February 2002.

[14] Smith, interviewed by the author, 16 February 2002; Francis, interviewed by the author, 14 February 2002; Ross, interviewed by the author, 18 February 2002; Schellenger, interviewed by the author, 5 February 2002.

The engine compartment of the X-31 illustrates a readily apparent difference between it and the HARV F-18. The X-31 has the individual vectoring paddle actuators and attachments as an integral part of the airframe, located at the top and lower left and right corners of the nacelle. These were built into the structure itself, something made possible because the airframe had been specifically designed for use in this research program. The HARV program's F-18, on the other hand, used an existing airframe and the vectoring paddles and actuators had to be attached to the plane's exterior.

than anyone expected. But the scale models did not incorporate the aircraft's flight control system and did not anticipate how hard that FCS would fight to regain control of the aircraft. When one of the full-scale X-31s actually went out of control at the end of the flight test program and the pilot ejected from the aircraft, one of the biggest surprises was that the unpiloted X-31's FCS actually regained an element of control before the aircraft departed controlled again and finally crashed.[15]

Perhaps the biggest setback during the construction phase of the X-31 occurred when one of the wing skins being manufactured by MBB was dropped, damaging it beyond repair. The skin from the second wing was removed and used to replace the damaged first skin, but the accident set the schedule back three months. Between that incident, the accumulated delays caused by the bottleneck with the Iron Bird for software integration, and assorted other small problems, the X-31 construction schedule slipped a full year. But finally, the first X-31, piloted by Rockwell test pilot Ken Dyson, lifted off the runway at Palmdale on 11 October 1990 for a successful first flight. The first flight of ship number 2 followed on 19 January 1991. The first international X-Plane had finally become a reality.[16]

The X-31 Move to Dryden

Phase III of the X-31 program, which primarily covered aircraft construction, also called for a limited flight test program at Rockwell's Palmdale facility before moving the aircraft to Patuxent River (casually referred to as "Pax River") for more detailed flight test and a tactical utility demonstration flight program. But as both aircraft moved past their first flights, two sizeable problems began to emerge.

The first involved Navy procedures for granting required clearances prior to each test flight. The Navy's clearance process, established primarily for production test flights and operational aircraft, was seen as unacceptably exacting and slow by Rockwell, MBB, and even DARPA. It took a full year to complete the conventional envelope clearance on the X-31, and every month the program dragged on, the greater the likelihood became that funding for the program would disappear, despite pressure by the Germans for its continuation. This funding crisis was the second and most critical problem faced in the program's early stages, and it began to emerge even before the X-31s took flight.

DARPA and Nunn-Quayle funds had been used to pay for the U.S. portion of designing and building the X-31, but by 1991 support within DARPA for the program had begun to wane. After supplying seed money, DARPA had expected one of the military services to buy into the effort and supply follow-on funding for the flight test program. Five years later, DARPA priorities had begun to shift, and the agency's managers began to question the worth of continued funding for a program that the military branches didn't seem especially interested in pursuing. So even as the X-31 planes took to the sky for the first time, the program was in real danger of being shut down.

The budget crunch made timely completion of flight tests even more important, and it also led Col. Tack Nix to begin looking for potential new partners to help keep the program afloat. In late 1990, Col. Nix began discussions with the Ames-Dryden Flight Research Facility (now Dryden Flight Research Center) about moving the X-31 flight test program to the NASA facility at Edwards Air Force Base in California.[17]

Moving the flight test program to NASA rather than to Patuxent River was attractive to DARPA and to the German Flight Test Agency (WTD-61) for several reasons. For one, the sunny weather in California's high desert would permit greater frequency of test flights, a major point of concern for schedule-pressed X-31 managers. Dryden also had an impressive flight test support system, including well-equipped mission control rooms and access to the wide-open Western Aeronautical Test Range at Edwards, as well as extensive flight test experience with unconventional

[15] "Roll-Out," 17-19; Robinson, interviewed by author, 14 February 2002; Edward H. Phillips, "NASA Langley Drop Model Explores X-31A High-Alpha, Post-Stall Flight," *Aviation Week & Space Technology*, 2 March 1992, 54-56.

[16] "X-31A: 'Barrier Breaker for the 21st Century," Rockwell document, DFRC Historical Reference Collection, 11.

[17] Letter from Guy M. See to Joe Gera regarding Tack Nix visit to discuss NASA participation in the X-31 program, 6 December 1990, DFRC Historical Reference Collection.

X-Plane designs. In addition, the X-31 would be a "big fish" in the NASA pond at Dryden, which could affect the amount of attention paid to the project and its needs. By contrast, the main focus at the Navy's Patuxent River facility was on flight test programs connected to higher-priority fleet aircraft. At Pax River the X-31 might have been relegated to a spot much lower on the priority list for resources and flight scheduling.

There was some hesitation among the industry partners about moving to NASA, however. NASA had developed something of a reputation, especially among Rockwell managers who had worked with Dryden on the HiMAT program, for sometimes getting so wrapped up in the intricate research details of a project that schedules and progress slowed to a standstill. On the other hand, engineers and crew at NASA would at least understand the non-production nature of the X-31, which would in turn allow the flight test program to proceed faster than the Navy had allowed in the X-31's first year of flight.[18]

The final advantage offered by a move to Dryden was financial. Patuxent River had switched to an "institutional" accounting system, which charged support staff and resources to individual programs rather than to the facility's general overhead. Dryden could absorb the costs of all its personnel and support services, saving the X-31 program an enormous amount of money. Over the course of the X-31 program's three years at Dryden, NASA contributed the equivalent of $14.9 million to the effort in "indirect" support.[19]

The decision to move the aircraft to Dryden was not a popular one with the Navy. To soften the blow, official plans continued to call for the aircraft to be relocated to Patuxent River for the tactical utility phase of the research program, once the PST maneuvering experiments and demonstrations had been completed at Dryden. But primarily because of costs involved in moving the program to Pax River, the aircraft remained at Dryden for the duration of the flight test program.

Not everyone at NASA was happy about the de-cision to move the X-31 program to Dryden, either. The X-31 program emphasis on demonstrating the utility of the aircraft for military tactical maneuvering struck many at Dryden as something better done by the military than NASA, because the program had only limited opportunities for the kind of pure data gathering that was the primary interest of many NASA researchers and the hallmark of NASA research efforts. Yet the X-31 offered the ability to study the dynamics of high-alpha flight that the X-29 and F-18 HARV aircraft lacked. The F-18 HARV may have had three-dimensional thrust-vectoring capability, but the X-31 did as well, and it had a 40 percent higher thrust-to-weight ratio, 35 percent lower wing loading, a 30 percent higher maximum normal load factor, and twice the thrust-vectoring control power of the F-18 HARV. These differences meant that the X-31 would be capable of much better dynamic maneuvers than the HARV. While NASA would have to work within the confines of the X-31 program's existing instrumentation and flight test objectives, participation would allow Dryden researchers to explore areas of high-alpha and thrust-vectored flight they couldn't reach with either the X-29 or the F-18 HARV.[20]

By the summer of 1991, DARPA officials had made the decision to move the X-31 program to Dryden and include NASA and the Air Force as partners in the research effort. On 20 January 1992, the two X-31 aircraft flew together from Palmdale to the Dryden facility at Edwards Air Force Base, which served as home for not only the aircraft but the entire X-31 International Test Organization (ITO) team for the next three years. Despite the original program goal of pitting the two X-31 aircraft against each other in simulated combat maneuvers, the ferry flight to Edwards turned out to be the only time the two ever flew together.[21]

---

[18] Schellenger, interviewed by the author, 5 February 2002; Fred Knox, interviewed by the author, 1 October 2001; Francis, interviewed by the author, 14 February 2002; Robinson, interviewed by the author, 27 March 2002; Kenneth J. Szalai, interviewed by the author, 6 March 2002; Ross, interviewed by the author, 18 February 2002; Joe Gera, interviewed by the author, 8 August 2001.

[19] Letter from Dr. E. Buchacker, X-31A Flight Test Coordinator for WTD-61 to Kenneth J. Szalai, 31 January 1991 regarding WTD-61's wish to have NASA involved in the X-31 flight test program, DFRC Historical Reference Collection; "X-31 Total Estimated Development Costs," document, 24 March 1995, DFRC Historical Reference Collection; Francis, interviewed by the author, 14 February 2002.

[20] "Flight Research Objectives of NASA in the X-31 Enhanced Fighter Maneuverability (EFM) Program," undated document, from the NASA Dryden Flight Research Center archives; Francis, interviewed by the author, 14 February 2002.

The ITO/ITF

Plans to bring the X-31 program to Dryden began in 1990 with Tack Nix's discussions with Dryden managers. The proposal was locate the X-31 program team in a new building under construction at the facility that was designed for better integration of research teams and research components. The new facility, called the Integrated Test Facility (ITF), was designed to support "hardware and software development, test, diagnosis, and qualification of advanced aircraft utilizing highly integrated flight/propulsion control systems."[22] The ITF also provided a place where program management, engineering support, simulation facilities, and the aircraft could be co-located.

As with any flight-research effort, simulation played an important role in developing software for the vehicle, predicting aircraft behavior, and training pilots prior to actual research flights. The X-31 used both real-time and batch simulations. Batch simulations were used for control-law development and flight data analysis, and real-time simulations were used for piloted evaluations, analysis, and software verification and validation. And while the X-31 program did not have a dedicated Iron Bird, the ITF facilities did allow the team to conduct Flight Hardware In Loop Simulation that employed actual flight-qualified flight control computers and the same redundancy-management features as used with the X-31.[23]

But the team couldn't take advantage of all these capabilities or even occupy its designated office spaces at Dryden until the ITF was completed. The building was to be ready for occupation in early 1991, and the X-31 team members were scheduled to be the building's first occupants. Because of construction delays, the building was not ready for occupancy until January 1992.[24]

The other major task facing the new X-31 team was to determine how numerous partners would work together, and the challenge was enough to overwhelm any program manager. The team now consisted not only of representatives from defense departments and contractors of two nations, but from government and industry, the U.S. Air Force and the U.S. Navy, NASA, and the German Luftwaffe as well as the German Flight Test Agency. The opportunities for turf battles and conflict among the differing philosophies, cultures, and egos were daunting.

The team set up an official ITO structure that tried, to the extent possible, to refrain from making any one pilot, engineer, or project manager the "chief" in charge, stressing instead cooperative decision-making and shared responsibility in all areas and encouraging team members to choose their own leaders in each research area. Even the official X-31 team logo was carefully designed in an elongated circle so that no organization would have "top" billing. There was an official hierarchy in the ITO structure, but Ken Szalai, then the Ames-Dryden facility director, advised team managers that if they would ever need to consult the complicated ITO organizational chart for purposes of conflict resolution, they would be in trouble. The only thing likely to guarantee success for such a complex team was voluntary cooperation and mutual respect, especially when it came to conflict resolution. Flexibility also was important; it took an unprecedented and unconventional management approach to make the ITO work. Contractors reported to civil servants and vice versa, and if team members had insisted on hard-and-fast adherence to conventional contractor/government interactions, the project would have failed.

It took awhile for mutual respect and trust to develop among ITO team members, but locating the team in the ITF helped. It also helped that senior managers were willing to replace individuals who didn't seem to be working well with other team members. Eventually, however, loyalty to the X-31 effort began to supersede the organizational loyalties team members brought to the research program. As Air Force Col. Mike Francis described it, the X-31 team "went from a dysfunctional

[21] "Flight Test Summary, Aircraft #1 and #2," flight log documents, 21 July 1995, from the NASA Dryden Flight Research Center archives; Francis, interviewed by the author, 14 February 2002.

[22] Letter from Ted Ayers to Col. John "Tack" Nix regarding Ames-Dryden interest in supporting the X-31 program, undated draft, DFRC Historical Reference Collection.

[23] Sheen, interviewed by the author, 11 March 2002; "X-31/JAST FMIPT Meeting," 16 November 1994, viewgraphs, DFRC Historical Reference Collection; Joe Gera, interviewed by the author, 8 August 2001; "X-31 Simulation/ITF Requirements," memo, from Dale Mackall to Dwain Deets, et. al, 30 August 1991, DFRC Historical Reference Collection.

[24] "X-31 Issues," undated (but clearly late 1991) viewgraphs, DFRC Historical Reference Collection.

high school football team, to a team of Super Bowl champions."[25]

Glitches and points of disagreement existed among team members, of course. Among the frustrations that Rockwell and MBB team members endured were three- and six-month delays, respectively, for resuming flight tests with the two X-31s at NASA while Dryden personnel inspected the aircraft and got acquainted with their systems. This served to reinforce concerns about NASA's reputation for giving more attention to exacting detail than to schedule pressures. As one Rockwell manager put it, "NASA's culture was, 'let's not be in a rush.' And we were in a rush." The rush was not simply impatience on the part of Rockwell and MBB. Delays cost money, and the X-31 program was constantly operating on "financial fumes," as one of its DARPA program managers described it. The longer the program lingered, the greater the chance it would be cancelled altogether. Finding the right balance among "safe," "perfect," and "good enough" was something the team battled constantly throughout its time at Dryden.[26]

Although program originators had always envisioned including demonstrations of tactical maneuvers in flight-test phases of the X-31 program, the actual MOA signed by the German and U.S. X-31 partners called only for demonstration of post-stall maneuvers. So in June 1992, the MOA was modified to include demonstration of combat maneuvers.[27]

The X-31 Flight Test Program

Once the ITO had been formulated and inspections of the aircraft were complete, a limited flight test program resumed with the first X-31 in late April 1992. The second X-31 flew again at the beginning of July. Soon after resuming envelope-expansion flights, researchers discovered a problem that wind tunnel tests had not predicted. At higher angles of attack, so much deflection was needed from the trailing-edge flaps for pitch control that the flaps lacked sufficient differential movement to provide adequate roll control.

The wind tunnel model, it turned out, had been mounted with two attach rods along the underside of the aft fuselage, contributing an unforeseen nose-down pitching moment. The actual X-31 didn't have these rods, and therefore lacked the nose-down influence they provided. But Langley wind tunnel researchers provided a quick and easy fix for the problem once the cause was identified. In the space of only one week, two aft strakes were designed, tested in wind tunnels, and fabricated for the aircraft. The four-foot strakes were made of plywood sandwiched between two metal pieces and covered with fiberglass. The nose-down pitch authority issue was resolved as soon as the ventral strakes were attached to each side of the tail section.

A more serious problem developed as researchers began expanding the flight envelope beyond steady-state high-alpha conditions. Researchers knew that in actual combat, fighter pilots would most likely enter the post-stall region at high speed and in an aggressive manner. So after determining the X-31's stability and control under steady-state, or 1g, conditions, researchers wanted to evaluate the aircraft's performance at high-speed dynamic entry into post-stall flight, where the forces and moments confronting the aircraft and its control system would be stronger.

The first time Air Force test pilot Lt. Col. Jim Wisneski attempted a dynamic entry up to 60 degrees alpha, the X-31 yawed abruptly and departed controlled flight. Wisneski quickly recovered control, but researchers knew the problem needed resolution before flight test could continue. The root of the problem turned out to be the extremely strong influence of asymmetries in the vortices coming off the aircraft's forebody at high angles of attack. Researchers discovered that the X-31 nose shapes were not quite as perfect, nor as rounded, as those on the wind tunnel models. The aircraft had already exhibited unsettling asymmetries between 45-55 degrees alpha, and the departure incident emphasized the need to improve

[25] Francis, interview, 14 February 2002; Smith, interviewed by the author, 16 February 2002; Gary Trippensee, interviewed by the author, 13 August 2002; Szalai, interviewed by the author, 6 March 2002; Ross, interviewed by the author, 18 February 2002.

[26] Francis, interview, 14 February 2002; Schellenger, interviewed by the author, 5 February 2002; Ross, interviewed by the author, 18 February 2002; John Perry, interviewed by the author, 6 February 2002; Szalai, interviewed by the author, 6 March 2002; Smith, interviewed by the author, 16 February 2002; "X-31 Flight Logs," DFRC Historical Reference Collection.

[27] "X-31: From Roll-out to Tactical Evaluation," Deutsche Aerospace document, April 1994, from Peter Huber personal files, 14.

An exterior view of the X-31's aft fuselage, highlighting the three thrust-vectoring paddles. While illustrating an extreme angle of deflection, the paddles are actually in repose. Without power, the airplanes's hydraulic system is unpressurized, allowing the paddles to be completely relaxed. Also visible is one of the strakes added to the airframe for increased control and stability. It runs from left to right in the photo, starting near the bottom of the airframe and ending at the hinge of the vectoring paddle.

performance and control. So in addition to installing small nose strakes on the X-31, the sharp noses of both aircraft were rounded off to help mitigate the vortices they created. "Grit strips" also were added to the noseboom and radome in an effort to influence the uniformity of these vortices.

As an added safety measure, the X-31 thrust-vectoring system was modified to allow a greater amount of thrust deflection, and therefore a greater amount of control. The deflection angle of the paddles had originally been limited to 27 degrees out of concern that the paddles might interfere with one another. That amount was increased to give the paddles the ability to deflect up to 34 degrees into the exhaust plume. The control laws also were modified to improve the control system's ability to respond to unusual sideslip movements or forces. Changes in control laws and control system software were not unusual in the course of the X-31 research. A total of 32 software releases were made during the program, most of which involved changes in control laws. But after modifications to the forebody,

control laws, and thrust-vectoring system were made, no further departures or surprising control problems occurred until the final flight of the X-31 program.[28]

[28] "X-31 Flight Logs," DFRC Historical Reference Collection; "X-31 Post-Stall Envelope Expansion and Tactical Utility Testing," presentation by Dave Canter, NAWC-AD, at the Fourth High Alpha Conference, NASA Dryden Flight Research Center, 13-14 July 1994, from NASA Conference Publication 10143, Volume 2; Brent R. Cobleigh, "High-Angle-of-Attack Yawing Moment Asymmetry of the X-31 Aircraft from Flight Test," NASA Contractor Report 186030, September 1994; Ross, interviewed by the author, 18 February 2002; Trippensee, interviewed by the author, 13 August 2002; Huber, interviewed by the author, 7 February 2002; Knox, interviewed by the author, 1 October 2001; Schellenger, interviewed by the author, 5 February 2002; Smith, interviewed by the author, 16 February 2002; Sheen, interviewed by the author, 11 March 26, 2002; "Yaw Control Prior to 2-73 Departure," Internal Rockwell International Letter from C.A. Crother to H. Schellenger, 11 December 1992, DFRC Historical Reference Collection; "X-31: From Roll-out to Tactical Evaluation," DASA document, April 1994, from Peter Huber personal files, 12-14; "X-31 Flight Test Update," SETP Conference Proceedings, September 1993, 100-109; Richard Hallion and Michael H. Gorn, *On the Frontier: Experimental Flight Research at NASA Dryden* (Washington, D.C.: Smithsonian Institution Press, 2003).

Herbst Maneuver

1. **X-31 enters maneuver at high speed (M 0.5 or greater)**

2. **X-31 decelerates rapidly while increasing angle of attack**

3. **X-31 exceeds conventional aerodynamic limit (stall) – needs thrust vectoring for control**

4. **Angle of attack increases to maximum of 70∞**

5. **X-31 rapidly pivots 180**

6. **X-31 lowers nose and accelerates to high speed**

7. **X-31 now flying in opposite direction**

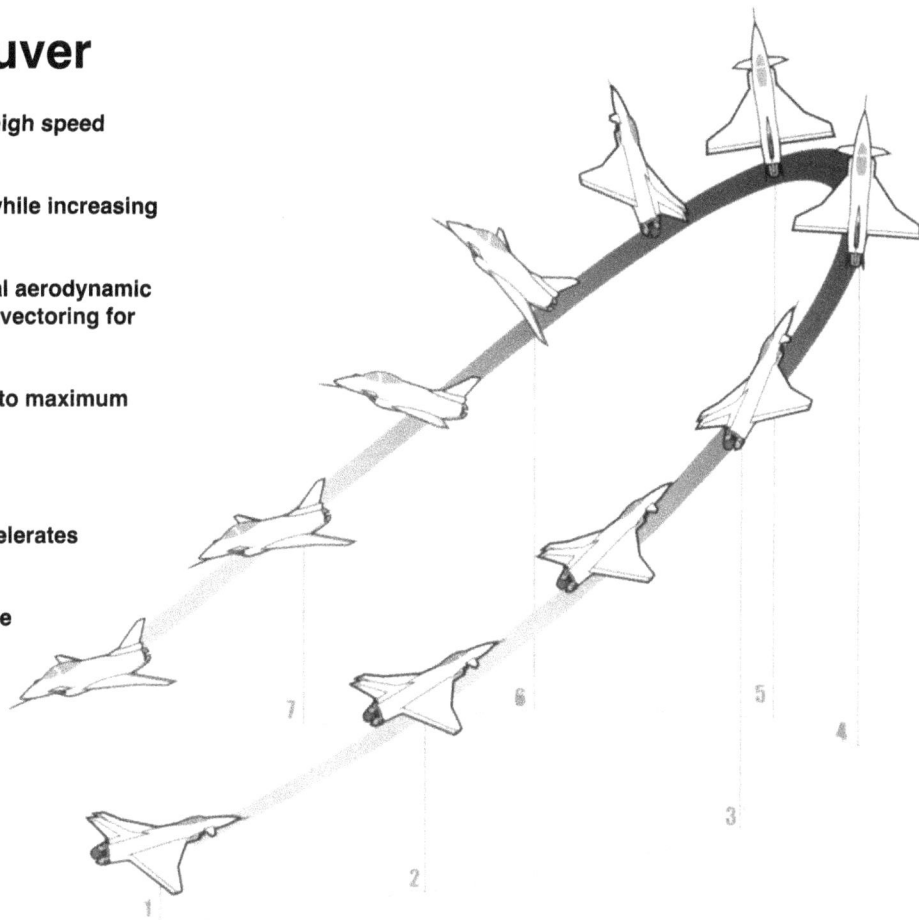

As with many research and development programs, the X-31 scheduling was probably over-optimistic. With time costing money, program managers felt pressured to present a "best-case" scheduling scenario, fully aware that the schedule would probably slip as problems arose. But as managers looked at the slow progress being made with the X-31 in expanding its post-stall flight envelope, they became concerned that the program would be forced to shut down before even reaching the tactical demonstration phase. In 1992, a marathon meeting attended by all X-31 program participants was held to try and reach a consensus on how to focus the goals of the post-stall flight test program more efficiently.

The result of that meeting was the establishment of four critical "Maneuver Milestones" that would constitute acceptable post-stall envelope-expansion benchmarks. The four milestones were:

1. Sustained equilibrium flight at 70 degrees alpha
2. A 360-degree velocity vector roll at 70 degrees alpha
3. Successful rapid, dynamic entry into deep post-stall conditions
4. Successful demonstration of a Herbst Maneuver

The "Herbst Maneuver" consisted of a heading reversal with a near-zero turn radius from and returning to high-speed flight. In essence, a Herbst Maneuver was the aerial equivalent of a swimmer performing a flip turn at the end of a lap in a swimming pool– something requiring controlled flight at extremely high angles of attack, and a maneuver conventional aircraft were incapable of executing.

By changing the envelope expansion approach from that of a traditional data matrix to one with a more streamlined, "milestone" focus, the research team condensed what some managers had projected would be a 10-year flight program (at the rate the program was going in 1992) into approximately nine months. On 29 April 1993, German test pilot Karl Lang successfully executed a Herbst Maneuver at a 70-degree angle of attack, marking the successful completion of the final post-stall maneuver milestone.[29]

Tactical Evaluation

With the post-stall envelope expansion completed, the X-31 team was ready to begin the program's

man Luftwaffe, who joined the X-31 cadre of pilots in March 1993 in order to give the Luftwaffe a better idea of how a thrust-vectored aircraft would perform in the hands of a trained combat pilot.

The original idea of having the X-31s fly mock combat against each other had been abandoned, so an F-18 was selected as the primary adversary aircraft. The tactical demonstrations were also limited to one-versus-one engagements.

Mock combat between two aircraft–one of them a rare research aircraft–presented a new and unique

Photographed from the chase plane at high angles of attack, the narrowed paddles and the extreme deflection of the fore planes are clearly visible on the X-31.

tactical evaluation phase. In preparation for the tactical demonstrations, the X-31 team conducted two extensive simulation programs at the IABG facility. The first, called "Pinball 1," took place in September and October 1991, and the second, "Pinball 2," took place in April 1993. The simulations were designed to develop both tactical maneuvers for the X-31 and rules of engagement for the tactical demonstrations. They also were used to train pilots and other support personnel who would be conducting the demonstration flights. Among the pilots trained in the simulations was Lt. Col. Quirin Kim, a fighter pilot from the Ger-

challenge for the Dryden research team. NASA had never performed such an extensive tactical evaluation. In addition to safety-of-flight concerns to be considered, there was also the basic need to integrate new instrumentation and real-time monitoring systems to determine the outcome of the engagements.

[29] Francis, interviewed by the author, 14 February 2002; "X-31: Post Stall Pioneer +," viewgraphs, from presentation by Francis, 14 February 2002; "X-31: From Roll-out to Tactical Evaluation," DASA document, April 1994, 14-15; "X-31 Enhanced Fighter Maneuverability Program Final Report, Volume 1," videotape recording.

After conducting a series of flight tests throughout the fall of 1993 to develop and evaluate basic fighter maneuvers with the X-31, pilots began tactical evaluation flights with the X-31 and one of NASA's F-18 aircraft. Initially, the F-18 exhibited better performance than the X-31 but when the F-18 was loaded with combat munitions, the two aircraft were fairly well matched. The goals of the demonstrations were to define tactics that might be useful or necessary to take advantage of thrust-vectoring capability, and also to evaluate its effectiveness in close-in combat situations.

military community was skeptical about their validity. Because some of the pilots flying the F-18s were test pilots, several critics suggested the difference was pilot experience, and they raised questions about other vagaries in the tests. To answer critics, the X-31 team suggested bringing in other fighter pilots and aircraft to compete against the X-31 in a "guest adversary" program. And so the next phase of the demonstrations, which took place in 1994, pitted the X-31 against other front-line U.S. fighters, including an F-14 Tomcat, an F-15 Eagle, and a fleet version F-18 Hornet. The

The X-31 in flight showing the deflecting canards and the thrust-vectoring nozzles in action.

The tactical demonstrations evaluated the X-31's performance in three combat scenarios: entering the conflict from an equal, or "line abreast" position; from a disadvantaged, or defensive position; and from an offensive position. The results surprised even the researchers. Based on the simulation results, they expected an approximately 3:1 kill ratio in the scenarios; the actual results were an order of magnitude better. Entering the conflict from an equal position, the X-31 scored a 30:1 kill ratio; from a defensive position, a 3:1 ratio. And the X-31 won 100 percent of the engagements where it started from an offensive position.

The results were so overwhelming, in fact, that the

results of the adversary program were comparable to the results against NASA's F-18. The only fleet fighter against which the X-31 did not fare as well was the Air Force's new, higher-performance F-16, which had a much greater thrust-to-weight ratio than the X-31. And even in that scenario, the F-16 pilot acknowledged that he had to modify his tactics to defeat the X-31, making the fight a vertical one in order to capitalize on his better thrust-to-weight capability.

Clearly, basic aircraft performance remained a critical factor in air-combat superiority. In addition, the tactical demonstrations evaluated only one-versus-one engagements; in multiple-bogey situations, the kill ratio undoubtedly would have been different. The tactics used by the X-31 pilots also mattered.[30] To maintain their advantage, the pilots had to use the thrust-vectoring intelligently so as to avoid ending at low altitude in a low-energy state. But the X-31 flights clearly demonstrated that the additional tool of thrust-vectoring could give a fighter a significant, or even critical, edge.[31]

X-31 Follow-On Programs

Despite the success of the tactical demonstrations, the X-31 program still did not won the support of the U.S. military. Although even the modified X-31 MOA did not take the program beyond the tactical demonstration phase, ITO managers at Dryden were eager to consider additional flight experiments, hoping to extend the program and perhaps provide additional results that might win support for the thrust-vectoring or super-maneuverability concepts. In December 1993, the official International X-31 MOA was modified to extend the program to incorporate some of these follow-on experiments.

Helmet Mounted Display

In 1992, the Air Force expressed interest in using the X-31 to test a new helmet mounted display (HMD) manufactured by General Electric Corp. Ltd. (GEC), United Kingdom. The helmet was designed to allow pilots to maintain better visual contact with an adversary while retaining access to the kind of critical flight information that was projected on a fixed Heads-Up Display (HUD).

The initial HMD was not rated favorably by the X-31 pilots. But GEC was developing a second HMD called the "Viper," which was monocular and included visor projection of information. The Viper display was tested in the second X-31 aircraft in close-in combat exercises and it performed well, and the pilots gave much more positive feedback about its use.

For their part, X-31 managers also saw in the Viper's visor projection display the opportunity to test the X-31 in mock combat scenarios against "virtual" computer-generated adversaries–something that would allow them to demonstrate the X-31's effectiveness against multiple bogeys. Since one of the arguments against the X-31's initial combat demonstration was that most real-life scenarios involved multiple adversaries, a "virtual adversary" program might have addressed that concern. Unfortunately, funding for the virtual adversary program never materialized.

Nevertheless, HMD flights with the X-31 did permit exploration of another point in the debate over the need for super-maneuverability in fighters. The advent of short-range missiles had been key to exploring super-maneuverability since in order to use the missiles it was necessary for a fighter to be pointed at the target within short range. But as missile technology developed, a debate emerged over whether it was better to make the missile platform (the aircraft) more maneuverable, or to simply make the missile more maneuverable. New, "off-boresight" missiles such as the AIM-9X offered a potential solution because they could be launched from a fighter pointed away from the target.

X-31 proponents, however, argued that while the new missiles were clearly a tremendous improvement, their efficacy could be further improved by making both the platform and the missile more maneuverable, since the missile's effectiveness deteriorated somewhat as the angle at which it had to turn toward the target after launch increased.

The question is still unresolved, but the HMD experiments with the X-31 at least allowed researchers to explore the potential combination of a maneuverable aircraft with a maneuverable missile.[32]

---

[30] "Bogey" is a term referring to "enemy" aircraft.

[31] "X-31 Enhanced Fighter Maneuverability Program Final Report, Volume 1," videotape record; Francis, interview, 14 February 2002; "X-31: Post Stall Pioneer +," viewgraphs, 14 February 2002; "X-31: From Roll-out to Tactical Evaluation," DASA document, April 1994; Cmdr. Al Groves, et. al, "X-31 Flight Test Update," Society of Experimental Test Pilots Thirty-seventh Symposium Proceedings, ISSN #0742-3705, September 1993, 100-109; D. Eubanks, et. al, "X-31 CIC Flight Test Results," viewgraphs, from Full Envelope Agility Workshop Briefing, Eglin AFB, Fla., March 1995, DFRC Historical Reference Collection.

[32] "X-31 Enhanced Fighter Maneuverability Program Final Report, Volume 1," videotape recording; Col. Michael Francis, USAF (Ret.), interviewed by the author, 14 February 2002; "X-31: Post Stall Pioneer +," viewgraphs, 14 February 2002; "X-31: From Roll-out to Tactical Evaluation," DASA document, April 1994, 30-32.

Quasi-Tailless Research

During the X-31 program, DARPA was working on possible technologies and design specifications for the next-generation U.S. military fighter. Through the Joint Advanced Strike Technologies (JAST) program, research was being conducted to explore possible new technologies that might be incorporated into what would become the Joint Strike Fighter (JSF) design.[33]

JAST managers were interested in thrust-vectoring technology, but not for extreme maneuverability. Their interest focused on whether the technology would foster improved carrier approaches by allowing a slower-speed, higher angle of descent, or a design with a lower radar signature. Thrust-vectoring had the potential to reduce an aircraft's radar signature because with the added yaw stability and control thrust-vectoring provided, a thrust-vectored aircraft could conceivably be designed with either a smaller vertical tail or even no tail at all.

In an effort to address Air Force concerns about the X-31's relevance, the team conducted demonstrations of thrust-vectoring at supersonic speeds in March 1994. In addition to demonstrating thrust-vectoring with the X-31 in a standard configuration, the X-31 also performed some "quasi-tailless" thrust-vectoring at both subsonic and supersonic speeds. The flights were called "quasi-tailless" because researchers intentionally programmed the X-31's flight control computer to counter the influence of its vertical tail and rudder, making the aircraft respond and fly as if it had either a reduced tail or no vertical tail at all. Researchers then used thrust-vectoring to compensate for the aircraft's resulting instability. In the supersonic quasi-tailless experiment, the FCC simulated a 70 percent reduction in vertical tail size. The X-31 had performed well in those tests, but JAST managers wanted to see how it performed in two higher-risk scenarios staged closer to the ground: simulated carrier approaches and simulated air-to-ground combat.

The JAST research, conducted during the fall of 1994, showed that the X-31 was capable of carrier approaches, formation flying, and air-to-ground maneuvers using only thrust-vectoring to stabilize the aircraft in yaw. Some issues needed further investigation, such as saturation of the thrust-vectoring system's control capability in situations with low speed and high roll accelerations. Some of this was undoubtedly due to the X-31's rudimentary paddle-dependent thrust-vectoring system, which was inefficient and which researchers suspected caused unwanted interaction between the vehicle aerodynamics and the thrust-vectoring system that a production, axisymmetric thrust-vectoring nozzle would not encounter. Researchers also acknowledged that a tailless aircraft dependent on thrust-vectoring for directional/yaw stability and control would need a reasonable backup system in the event of engine failure. The backup approach used by the X-31 was its moveable canard, which could be canted down into the airflow to give the pilot enough nose-down pitch authority to regain aerodynamic control in the event of an engine flameout, allowing the pilot to attempt an air restart. Although engineers hoping to design an operational tailless fighter would have some issues to resolve, the X-31 experiments clearly demonstrated the feasibility of controlling and operating a fighter design with either a reduced or eliminated vertical tail.

Despite the success of these experiments, however, when the JSF requirements were released to potential bidders in the design competition, the specifications noted that the design could not be dependent on a working thrust-vectoring system for basic stability and control of the aircraft.[34]

X-31 Accident

As 1994 drew to a close, the X-31 program also was winding down. In addition to the quasi-tailless, helmet display, and adversary tactical demonstration

[33] DARPA is the acronym for the Defense Advanced Research Projects Agency. MBB also became part of Deutsche Aerospace (DASA) during the X-31 program and is now part of European Aeronautic Defence and Space Company (EADS). But to try to keep readers from getting lost in the permutations of alphabet soup among the program partners, I chose to continue to call the two partners DARPA and MBB in references throughout this chapter.

[34] John T. Bosworth and C. Stoliker, "The X-31A Quasi-Tailless Flight Test Results," NASA Technical Paper 3624, June 1996; Francis, interviewed by author, 14 February 2002; Schellenger, interviewed by the author, 5 February 2002; Robinson, interviewed by the author, 27 March 2002; Trippensee, interviewed by the author, 13 August 2001; "X-31 Enhanced Fighter Maneuverability Program Final Report, Volume 1," videotape record; "X-31: Post Stall Pioneer +," viewgraphs, 14 February 2002; "X-31: From Roll-out to Tactical Evaluation," DASA document, April 1994, 30-32.

flights, work on the program included flight experiments to compare the parameter identification and high-alpha handling characteristics with those of the F-18 HARV. Interestingly, the X-31 did not perform as well in terms of handling characteristics at high angles of attack during the Standard Evaluation Maneuvers (STEMS) and handling evaluations as it did in close-in combat scenarios. Evaluation pilots noted, however, that the maneuvers for research were different than those required for the close-in combat tasks.[35] But DARPA officials had decided not to fund the virtual adversary program, and all other research efforts were nearing completion. On 19 January 1995, German pilot Karl Lang took the X-31 number 1, tail number 584, out for the third sortie of the day and what was supposed to be the final flight of the X-31 program.

Unusual weather conditions prevailed on the day of the flight; as opposed to most days in California's high desert, the 19th of January was overcast, with higher-than-normal humidity. But the maneuvers to be performed were routine parameter identification experiments. After completing the flight, and as he was returning to base, Lang commented over the radio that the angle of attack and airspeed were not correlating. It was the first sign of a problem. A short time later, no doubt because of the irregularity reflected in his air data instruments, Lang told mission control crew members that he was turning on the pitot heat.

A pitot tube is one element of an instrument that records an aircraft's airspeed. It is usually a narrow tube projecting forward from the fuselage or wing, and on experimental aircraft such as the X-31 the pitot tube often extends forward from the nose of the aircraft into undisturbed air. If ice from moisture in the air forms within it, the pitot tube will potentially provide incorrect information since the ice will change the inner diameter of the tube and affect airflow through it. The X-31 had been outfitted with a special research "Kiel" probe to record its air data, a single-string system that meant the plane had no backup air data system. The Kiel probe was more accurate than standard pitot tube air data recording systems at high angles of attack, which is why it had been installed on the X-31. But it lacked a heating element, and when Lang announced that he was turning on what he thought was the pitot heat, no one on the ground either corrected him or understood that his comment might indicate a developing

problem.

A few minutes later, as Lang was running through his checklist to reconfigure the aircraft for landing, he remarked that he wanted to leave the pitot heat on a little longer. At that point the ground controller noted that the pitot heat was not connected, eliciting a laconic response from Lang. While the signs of impending trouble were easily recognized in hindsight, nobody realized what was happening as events began to unfold. Shortly after that transmission, the X-31 pitched up and did not respond to Lang's nose-down control inputs. Lang, as well as all other X-31 test pilots, had seen Langley's drop-model tests illustrating how violently the X-31 would react if it went out of control, so when the X-31 departed controlled flight and did not respond to his input, Lang made the decision to eject.

He parachuted safely to the ground and the X-31 crashed just north of Edwards Air Force Base. And although the accident was a terrible blow to everyone in the program, DARPA X-31 program manager Mike Francis called it the "most prolific data-gathering flight of the X-31 program," even though it was also, arguably, the most expensive one, resulting in the loss of a $100 million aircraft. Francis' comments referred to the fact that because the X-31 was so well instrumented, it telemetered data about its gyrations to researchers all the way to the ground.

Because of the volume of data produced, it did not take accident investigators long to determine the cause of the crash. The overcast, unusually humid conditions had, in fact, caused formation of ice in the Kiel probe, and this led the probe to generate inaccurate airspeed data. The discrepancy Lang reported between the X-31's angle of attack and what the airspeed typically read in that configuration was due to this error. This error was critical because the flight control system had different "gains," or responses, programmed into it for different airspeeds. At slow airspeeds, the Flight Control System (FCS) would command larger inputs to the control surfaces for a specific pilot command than it would at higher speeds, where reduced deflection of

---

[35] "X-31 Flight Logs," DFRC Historical Reference Collection; P.C. Stoliker, "High-Angle-of-Attack Handling Qualities Predictions and Criteria Evaluation for the X-31A," NASA TM 4758, March 1997; Patrick C. Stoliker and John T. Bosworth, "Evaluation of High-Angle-of-Attack Handling Qualities for the X-31A Using Standard Evaluation Maneuvers," NASA TM 104322, September 1996.

surfaces was required in order to achieve a specified aircraft response. The X-31 was going significantly faster than the Kiel probe indicated, leading the FCS to command control inputs too great for the actual flight condition. As the problem worsened the excess control movements caused the aircraft to depart controlled flight. To their surprise, researchers watching the X-31 descend to the ground after Lang ejected saw the FCS struggling to regain control of the aircraft, even stabilizing it briefly several times before the aircraft again departed controlled flight, flipped inverted, and spun into the ground.

Researchers acknowledge that the accident did not have to happen. Certainly, had the Kiel probe been heated or had there been a secondary air data system, the crash could have been avoided. But even with the X-31's existing system, there were ways the accident might have been averted. There were indications of trouble several minutes before the crash that, had anyone realized what those indications suggested, could have allowed corrective action to be taken in time. If the air-to-air radio communication system between the F-18 chase plane and the X-31 had been better (the chase pilot could hear the ground controller's communication with the X-31, but not the pilot's "hot mike" transmissions to the ground), the chase pilot probably would have noticed the discrepancy between the F-18's airspeed and what Lang was reporting. And finally, the X-31 was equipped with a manual override system for the FCS, as a system-malfunction contingency. There were three pilot-selectable flight modes, one of which would command a single level of gain response to the control surfaces. The aircraft would be far less capable in that configuration, but had Lang thought to select that reversionary mode, he could have brought the X-31 back to a safe landing. Despite this, even in retrospect such a scenario remains unlikely since

nearly everyone thought they had an airplane operating reasonably well right up to the point of departure from controlled flight.

All the Monday morning quarterbacking, however, could not change the fact that the X-31 had been lost. Fortunately, the pilot had survived, but it was a shocking and disheartening end to what had been an exceptionally successful flight test program.[36]

Paris Air Show

Early in the X-31 program, managers had discussed the possibility of taking the X-31 to the 1995 Paris Air Show to demonstrate its impressive capabilities for the public. After the loss of the first X-31 the team became much more interested in making the trip, for no one wanted the program to end with the black mark of an accident. The issue of collective personal pride aside, there was concern over the negative impact that ending the program with an accident might have on the eventual adoption of the X-31 technology, even though the accident had nothing to do with the thrust-vectoring system or the aircraft's inherent design.

The obstacles to getting the remaining X-31 to the Paris show, however, were significant. Funds for taking the X-31 to the show were not in the program's budget. Initial costs for the trip were estimated at around $2.4 million. The X-31's DARPA program manager convinced each of the four major partners in the X-31 program (Rockwell, MBB, the German government, and DARPA) to contribute $600,00 apiece to cover the costs.[37] The expenses included removing the X-31's wings and packing the aircraft into a cargo plane for transport to Germany, where it would be reassembled. This was necessary because, among other things, the X-31 had not been built with air-to-air refueling capability. The aircraft would have lacked the range to make the flight to Paris, even if the team had been willing to see the X-31 flown over the ocean.

Time, or lack thereof, was another concern. The Paris Air Show was in June, less than five months after the accident. The second X-31 was grounded for nearly 12 weeks after the incident while the crash investigation was conducted and the resulting safety

[36] Szalai, interviewed by the author, 6 March 2002; Francis, interviewed by the author, 14 February 2002; "X-31 Flight Logs," DFRC Historical Reference Collection; "X-31 Enhanced Fighter Maneuverability Program Final Report, Volume 1," videotape recording; "NASA X-31 Mishap Investigation Report," 18 August 1995, DFRC Historical Reference Collection; "NASA X-31 Mishap Investigation," viewgraphs, from briefing by Guy Gardner, Board Chairperson, to Ken Szalai, Director, Dryden Flight Research Center, 2 March 1995; "Radio Transcript from X-31 Accident," DFRC Historical Reference Collection; Schellenger, interviewed by the author, 5 February 2002.

[37] Michael A. Dornheim, "Paris Flight to Cap Busy X-31 Test Schedule," *Aviation Week & Space Technology*, 12 June 1995, 112; Francis, interviewed by the author, 14 February 2002.

recommendations were implemented. Not surprisingly, the accident investigation committee demanded that the second X-31 be equipped not only with pitot heat, but also with new software that would detect erroneous air data inputs at specified flight conditions.

Even with those changes, however, flying extreme maneuvers for an air show was a very different endeavor than performing maneuvers in the course of test flights. Air-show maneuvers were flown tight, close in, and low to the ground. The X-31 had never maneuvered below 15,000 feet. Its envelope would have to be expanded and cleared down to 500 feet–an altitude that increased the risk of maneuvers significantly, especially given that the X-31 was a single-engine aircraft. In addition, the X-31 pilots were test pilots and fighter pilots, not air-show pilots. To fly a demonstration at Paris would require different techniques than had been used in test flights. All this practice and envelope expansion would take time, even with extensive use of the X-31's simulator to develop maneuvers and link them into a final demonstration sequence and to allow pilots to practice both maneuvers and recoveries from potential system failures.[38]

The effort was complicated by the fact that U.S. Commerce Secretary Ron Brown had recently declined a request by NASA's administrator for funds to cover NASA's appearance at the Paris Air Show. Consequently, instructed not to officially support or attend the show, Dryden Center Director Ken Szalai's solution was to continue supporting the preparation efforts under the guise of "further envelope expansion." He also approved travel requests to send the NASA X-31 team members and pilots to the show, although they couldn't officially participate in events there. As a result, Rogers Smith, NASA's lead research pilot on the X-31 program, would support the X-31's aerial demonstrations from Le Bourget's control tower rather than performing them himself.

But while Szalai shared the team's desire to take the remaining X-31 to Paris, he was only willing to stick his neck out and support the effort financially if the team were really able to meet an overall deadline he'd imposed. He had team members submit a list of the lower-level and preliminary deadlines they believed it necessary to meet in order to make the larger goal of getting the plane to Paris on time. One of the first deadlines involved changes to the X-31's flight control software. After several weeks of long hours and even overnight sessions in Dryden's Integrated Test Facility, engineers were exhausted, and toward the end of one week they realized that they were likely to miss the first milestone deadline. They came close, but weren't able to complete the software changes in time. The engineers and pilots begged Szalai for an extension, but he closed the effort down and sent the team home. His reasoning was twofold. First, he wanted to force the team to get some rest so they could think through their problems more clearly. Second, Szalai knew that the schedule truly had no room for slack. If the team wanted the program to continue, they would have to come up with a convincing, workable alternative that would get the show schedule back on track.

The solution came from MBB's Hannes Ross, who flew to California to try and sway Szalai. Ross told Szalai he'd arranged for an Airbus Beluga to transport the X-31 directly to Paris. The Beluga was significantly larger in diameter than the C-5 Galaxy transport the team had planned to use to transport the X-31, so the plane wouldn't have to be disassembled and reassembled. It could be transported intact directly to Le Bourget, saving an entire week. What Ross *didn't* say was that the cost of using the Beluga would be around $750,000–funds the program didn't have. But the argument was enough to convince Szalai to allow the X-31's air show effort to continue. Fortunately, the cost of the Beluga never had to be addressed because the team managed to meet its deadlines before the X-31 was ready to leave Edwards, enabling them to use the C-5 transport after all.[39]

In addition to modifying the maneuvers to be performed with the X-31, the team removed the plane's spin chute and replaced it with a drag chute. The air-show maneuvers would be performed at too low a level for a spin chute to be of use, but the runway at Le Bourget was much shorter than those at Palmdale

[38] Fred D. Knox and Thomas C. Santangelo, "Taking an X-Airplane to the Paris Air Show," presentation to The Society of Experimental Test Pilots (Beverly Hills, CA: 29 September 1995), 3-5.

[39] Szalai, interviewed by the author, 6 March 2002; Francis, interviewed by the author, 14 February 2002; Ross, interviewed by the author, 18 February 2002; Smith, interviewed by the author, 16 February 2002.

or Edwards, and the X-31 had a landing speed of 170 knots. As Rockwell test pilot Fred Knox, who flew half of the demonstrations at Paris, noted dryly, "it was more important to stop than to stop spinning."[40]

On 20 May 1995, just four months after the first X-31 crashed, the second X-31 was put aboard a C-5 Galaxy and flown to Manching, Germany. Two weeks later, Rockwell test pilot Fred Knox flew the reassembled X-31 to Le Bourget, and on 10 June 1995 the X-31 took to the air for the public, "upstaging everything else there with heart-stopping aerobatic maneuvers."[41]

Pilots Knox and Kim took turns performing the daily X-31 demonstrations at the show. The demonstrations included a Herbst maneuver, a "Mongoose" maneuver, which was essentially a skidding post-stall turn, and post-stall loops with single- and double-heading reversals. The X-31's ability to sustain post-stall flight easily bested the "Cobra" maneuvers demonstrated by the Russians at the 1989 Paris show, and the demonstrations, conducted without incident at low altitude, definitively closed the debate over whether post-stall maneuvering was possible or controllable. The "stall barrier" that defined the bottom end of conventional aircraft flight envelopes had been broken, and it had been done in dramatic fashion before an international public audience. Reporters and military brass that had been briefed repeatedly about the X-31 during its flight test program reported that they didn't really understand the capabilities of the X-31 until the Paris demonstration. And the sale of several F-15s to Egypt at the show was reportedly made contingent on inclusion of an option for future modifications that would upgrade the aircraft to include thrust-vectored engines.[42]

Under any circumstances, the Paris demonstration would have been impressive. But coming as it did a mere four and a half months after losing one of the two X-31 aircraft in a crash, the success was nothing short of spectacular.

Conclusion

The Paris Air Show demonstration came almost 20 years after Dr. Wolfgang Herbst began arguing for the advantages and possibilities of post-stall flight. Sadly, the grandfather of the PST concept did not live to see his vision realized. Herbst died in an airplane accident only two months before the X-31 successfully demonstrated post-stall flight for the first time.

But even without Herbst, the X-31 program went on to accumulate an impressive list of accomplishments. It was the first international X-Plane program, one that successfully, if not effortlessly, blended a difficult and diverse combination of partners—a combination that evolved as the program progressed. It successfully demonstrated at least one approach to low-cost prototyping through the use of existing technology and fly-away tooling, and the streamlined management structure made famous by Lockheed's "Skunk Works." The X-31 program totaled approximately $230 million in direct costs, or about 60 percent of the X-29 program, yet had almost 50 percent more flights than did the X-29 program. In fact, the X-31 achieved the highest sortie rate of any X-Plane in a number of categories: 524 flights in 52 months, 580 in the entire program, 33 in one month, and 13 in one week.[43] It successfully demonstrated both conventional and quasi-tailless supersonic thrust-vectoring, and illustrated the distinct advantage thrust-vectoring could give a fighter pilot in close-in combat so long as the capability was used intelligently.

Moving the X-31 program to Ames-Dryden complicated the team structure, created delays while NASA personnel got up to speed on the aircraft and the program, and caused some friction over operational and flight clearance procedures. But overall, it was an extremely important and helpful move. On one front, it provided critical cost support at a time when the program was in real danger of being shut down for lack of funding. NASA's facilities and expertise also offered the X-31 team dedicated flight-research and

[40] Knox, interviewed by the author, 1 October 2001; Perry, interviewed by the author, 6 February 2002.

[41] "1996 Design & Engineering Awards," *Popular Mechanics*, January 1996, 45-48.

[42] "1995 X-31 Paris Air Show Trip Report," memo, from John T. Bosworth to acting chief, Research Engineering Division, Dryden Flight Research Center, 18 July 1995, DFRC Historical Reference Collection; Smith, interviewed by the author, 16 February 2002; Francis, interviewed by the author, 14 February 2002.

[43] "X-31 Program Close-Out Briefing," viewgraph presentation to Dr. Robert Whitehead, Associate Administrator of Aeronautics, NASA, 3 November 1995.

data-reduction capabilities that played a large role in the ability of the ITO team members to work together, to conduct as many research flights as they did, and to quickly solve the numerous technical problems that arose in the course of the X-31 research.[44]

The individual managers and leaders of the ITO played a vital role in that success, of course. Indeed, the template the organization provided for how to organize and execute a successful international or multi-partner research effort was as important as any of the program's technical achievements. If not for the co-location of team members, the unconventional shared-management structure of the program, and a general agreement among team members to put loyalty to the project ahead of individual turf concerns, the X-31 program would have been, at best, far less successful than it was.

In recognition of the program's significant accomplishments, the X-31 ITO was awarded the AIAA Reed Aeronautics Award (posthumously), to Dr. Herbst. It also won the Smithsonian Institution Air & Space Museum Trophy for Current Achievement in 1995 and the Ehrennadel der Deutschen Luftfahrt (the German Aerospace Society Award for Aeronautics Achievement) in 1996–the first time that award was given to an entire research team. The team also twice received an *Aviation Week & Space Technology* Laurels Award and a 1996 Design & Engineering Award from *Popular Mechanics*.[45]

The long-term impact of the technological advances explored and/or proven by the X-31 program is harder to judge. Some of the lessons Rockwell engineers learned about building a low-cost prototype aircraft, such as utilizing fly-away tooling and making best use of a geographically dispersed development team, were put to use in the development of the Boeing entry in the JSF design competition, the X-32.

The US Air Force adopted two-dimensional thrust vectoring on the F-22 Raptor (up and down), which is accomplished with paddles that are part of the exhaust nozzle. The F-35 Joint Strike Fighter also employs thrust vectoring on the short-take-off-and-landing version. In this case the entire exhaust nozzle swivels 90 degrees, from horizontal to straight down. At the time of this writing these were the only two US military production aircraft employing thrust vectoring.

To date, no U.S. or European military fighter has had thrust-vectoring incorporated into its design, although the technology has been considered for several designs and is still being considered for the Tranche 3 version of the Eurofighter.[46] But that isn't to suggest there is no interest in the thrust-vectoring concept.

Although the X-31 program harnessed thrust-vectoring to allow a fighter aircraft to maneuver easily in the post-stall region of flight, the U.S. military has shown an interest in thrust-vectoring not for extreme maneuverability, but for Extremely Short Take Off and Landing (ESTOL). The X-31's impressive display at the Paris Air Show got the attention of the Navy's senior management, which began discussions on how thrust-vectoring might be brought to bear in improving the safety of carrier takeoffs and landings. In January 2000, the X-31 was taken out of storage at Patuxent River and restored to flight status for a follow-on flight test program called Vectoring ESTOL Control Tailless Operation Research (VECTOR). On 24 February 2001, after a hiatus of five and a half years, the X-31 took to the air once again.

The VECTOR program is another joint U.S.-German effort among the U.S Navy, Boeing (which incorporates what was once Rockwell), the German WTD-61 test center, BWB (the German Federal Office for Defense Technology and Procurement), and DLR (the German Aerospace Research Agency). The goal of the VECTOR program is to explore the use of thrust-vectoring to allow slower, steeper approaches to aircraft carriers. The VECTOR program also is evaluating advanced Flush Air Data Systems (FADS), because existing air data collection systems are either problematic at high angles of attack or incompatible with an operational fighter's radome. In addition, the program was initially designed to encompass tailless research with the X-31 in which the aircraft's verti-

---

[44] "X-31: Post Stall Pioneer +," viewgraphs, from presentation by Francis, 14 February 2002.

[45] "X-31 Program Close-Out Briefing," viewgraph presentation to Dr. Robert Whitehead, Associate Administrator of Aeronautics, NASA, 3 November 1995; "1996 Design & Engineering Awards," *Popular Mechanics*, January 1996, 45-48.

[46] Ross, interviewed by the author, 18 February 2002; "X-31 Questions," Hannes Ross, email to Lane Wallace, 17 February 2002.

cal tail would be removed altogether, but funding restrictions relegated that part of VECTOR research to a paper study.[47]

The X-31 program made important contributions to the knowledge base available to designers and decision makers debating those options. The X-31 broke new ground in demonstrating what was possible in terms of thrust-vectored aircraft control and post-stall maneuvering–an envelope and area of flight research still being expanded and explored. And even if extreme maneuverability never becomes a driving design requirement for fighters, the X-31 research enabled the Navy to consider making safer aircraft carrier approaches and has removed at least some of the cultural and technical impediments to tailless aircraft designs–applications which may, ultimately, be elements that will drive the incorporation of thrust-vectoring into more military aircraft.

[47] "X-31 Experimental Aircraft Flies Again at Pax River," *Aerospace Daily*, 28 February 2001; Jennifer Young, interviewed by the author, 25 October 2001; Tom Lawrence, interviewed by the author, 21 September 2002; Robinson, interviewed by the author, 27 March 2002.

Chapter Four
The F-15 ACTIVE

Even before the X-31 and the F-18 HARV took to the skies, researchers already were looking to the next phase in thrust-vectoring research. Both the X-31 and F-18 HARV used a rudimentary thrust-vectoring system that relied on aft-end paddles to vector engine thrust. But researchers and manufacturers knew that if thrust-vectoring were ever to be incorporated into a production aircraft, a lighter and more workable system would have to be developed–a system that would likely rely on more highly integrated engine and flight control and some type of gimballing exhaust nozzle to vector the aircraft's engine exhaust in pitch and yaw.

Pratt & Whitney (P&W) and General Electric (GE), the two principal U.S. manufacturers of turbine engines for fighter jets, had begun working in the late 1980s with engine designs that featured multi-axis, axisymmetric thrust-vectoring nozzles. In the 1990s, two research programs evaluated these designs in flight. The first, known as the F-16 Multi-Axis Thrust-Vectoring (MATV) program, was a relatively short flight-research effort running between 1992-1993, and sponsored by General Dynamics, General Electric, and the U. S. Air Force Laboratories. In it, the Air Force's NF-16D Variable Stability In-flight Simulator Test Aircraft (VISTA) was retrofitted with a production-representative, multi-axis thrust-vectoring version of General Electric's F110-GE-100 engine.[1] The goal of the MATV program, like that of X-31 research, was to evaluate the tactical maneuvers that such a system would enable a fighter (in this case, an F-16) to accomplish. Like the F-18 HARV and the X-31 projects, research in the MATV program focused on the high-angle-of-attack, or post-stall, region of flight and, as with the X-31, on tactical application of thrust-vectoring technology. But a paddle-based thrust-vectoring system was used on the X-31, and the program investigated only one-versus-one combat scenarios in actual flight. The F-16 MATV used

a more sophisticated vectoring nozzle and evaluated both one-versus-one and one-versus-two engagements (although supersonic thrust-vectoring was not attempted with the MATV, as it was with the X-31).

The MATV program was under tight time constraints because the program had access to the VISTA F-16 for only a year. So, as one program briefing described it, "elegant approaches to flight control law and handling qualities development had to be sacrificed."[2] Ground simulation was limited, and researchers did not dwell on trying to understand the aerodynamic phenomena at high angles of attack. But in terms of the project's goal–demonstrating the potential tactical utility of retrofitting an existing fighter with a thrust-vectoring engine–the MATV program was extremely successful.

GE's axisymmetric nozzle was much more efficient than the paddles used on the F-18 HARV and the X-31, and the F-16's F110-GE-100 engine had significantly more thrust than the F404-GE-400, the type of engine in the HARV and X-31. Consequently, the F-16 MATV testbed could accomplish more dramatic maneuvers than the other two aircraft, sustaining angles of attack up to 85 degrees. And like the X-31 pilots, MATV pilots found that, used correctly, thrust-vectoring could give a fighter pilot a significant advantage in close-in combat.[3]

Meanwhile, engineers at Pratt & Whitney also had begun work on an axisymmetric thrust-vectoring nozzle. The P&W design evolved from the standard F100 axisymmetric balanced-beam nozzle (BBN), and retained most of the same components except in the final, divergent section of the nozzle. By adding extra static structure, a synchronization ring, and a hydraulic flap actuation system to the divergent section, designers created a nozzle that could articulate up to 20 degrees in any direction at a rate of 120 degrees or more per second (that rate, however, was limited

[1] The term 'production representative' indicates an item that will conform to production specifications but which is not yet in production. The item is thus beyond the developmental stage and occupies a middle ground in the process.

[2] Joseph E. Sweeney and Major Michael A. Gerzanics, "F-16 Multi-Axis Thrust-vectoring Program," presentation to the Thirty Seventh Symposium of The Society of Experimental Test Pilots, (Beverly Hills, CA: September 1993), 175.

[3] Ibid., "F-16 Multi-Axis Thrust-vectoring Program," 165-191; Joseph E. Sweeney and Major Michael A. Gerzanics, "F-16 MATV Envelope Expansion," presentation to the Thirty Eighth Symposium of The Society of Experimental Test Pilots, (Beverly Hills, CA: September 1994), 285-300.

to 80 degrees per second in flight tests), and at engine power settings from idle to full afterburner. The nozzle system also was designed with both hydraulic and electrical redundancy, with the idea of giving the system the capacity to perform flight-critical functions. The synchronization ring was designed with the capability of moving fore and aft along the engine centerline. This gave the engine the unique ability to adjust the nozzle area ratio (the difference between the throat area, where the synchronization ring was located, and the exit area of the nozzle). While not required for thrust-vectoring, this additional improvement to the F110-GE-100 engine allowed researchers to use adjustments in nozzle area ratio as yet another control effector that could be changed to improve aircraft performance or even alter the engine's noise footprint in flight.[4]

Pratt & Whitney engineers hoped to perform a flight test program with their new design, both to verify the nozzle's performance and to help demonstrate and sell the concept to the military. P&W already was working with McDonnell Douglas and the Air Force on the F-15 STOL Maneuverability Technology Demonstrator (S/MTD) program, which incorporated the use of a two-dimensional nozzle for pitch vectoring, and completed flight testing in September 1991. In the course of those experiments, S/MTD program managers from the Air Force, McDonnell Douglas and Pratt & Whitney began discussing the possibility of using the same aircraft to test P&W's new axisymmetric nozzle design. The group drew up a one-page document that listed project goals and requirements–a document that became the fundamental outline for the Advanced Control Technology for Integrated Vehicles (ACTIVE) program.[5]

The goals of the F-15 ACTIVE program were very different from those of other thrust-vectoring research programs being conducted during the same period. The F-18 HARV program had used thrust-vectoring to investigate the complex aerodynamics of high-alpha flight. Thrust-vectoring had been used in the X-31 and F-16 MATV to explore the ultimate application and tactical maneuvering benefits of the technology. Researchers in the F-15 ACTIVE program, by contrast, sought to understand the forces, moments, loads, and effectiveness of a specific thrust-vectoring system and explore ways the technology might be used to both improve the overall performance and efficiency of an aircraft and enable radically different aircraft designs.[6]

The programs' goals also differed in the region of flight probed by each. The F-18 HARV and the X-31 focused on slow-speed, high-angle-of-attack flight conditions, in which engines would be at high power and other forces on the aircraft would be minimized, and also used very rudimentary thrust-vectoring systems. ACTIVE researchers wanted to test a production-type nozzle in a much higher-speed, lower-alpha flight regime to determine performance benefits and controllability throughout a fighter's entire flight envelope. And while other programs, including that involving the Air Force F-16 MATV, had stressed aircraft maneuverability, ACTIVE researchers sought to evaluate other types of performance benefits, such as engine efficiency and noise reduction.

Two of the main objectives of the F-15 ACTIVE program, in fact, revolved around propulsion performance testing. By directly measuring the thrust, efficiency, and performance of the propulsion system, researchers hoped to evaluate not only the benefits and effectiveness of thrust-vectoring but also real-time performance–enhancing algorithms and technology. Two of these sensor/software systems were flight tested on the ACTIVE aircraft. The first, called the High Stability Engine Control (HISTEC), was an attempt to sense the actual airflow and distortion of air going into the engine in order to maximize engine performance without causing a stall. The second, called Adaptive Aircraft Performance Technology (AdAPT), sought to maximize the aircraft's power or range performance by sensing, in real time, any excess control or engine power and adjusting the aircraft and engine controls accordingly.

The ACTIVE program also was designed to focus much more closely on the dynamics and effectiveness

---

[4] Doane, et. al, "F-15 ACTIVE: A Flexible Propulsion Integration Testbed," AIAA paper 94-3360, presented at the 30th AIAA/ASME/SAE/ASEE Joint Propulsion Conference (Indianapolis, IN: 27-29 June 1994), 1-4; Roger Bursey, "The F-15 ACTIVE Aircraft, 'The Next Step,'" final draft of AIAA paper, 1995, DFRC Historical Reference Collection; Gerard Schkolnik, interviewed by the author, 25 April 2002; Roger Bursey, interviewed by the author, 26 April 2002.

[5] Schkolnik, interviewed by the author, 8 May 2001.

[6] Ibid.

of thrust-vectoring. The flight control software used in other thrust-vectoring research made separation of pure thrust-vectoring control from aerodynamic control inputs either difficult or impossible. ACTIVE researchers wanted to isolate aerodynamic and thrust-vectoring controls in order to better evaluate the performance of the thrust-vectoring, as well as to explore the feasibility of future aircraft designs that might rely solely on thrust-vectoring for control. In addition, ACTIVE researchers wanted to examine more closely the operation, dynamics, and effectiveness of Pratt & Whitney's thrust-vectoring nozzle design. The nozzle involved a mechanical system so complicated that researchers were unable to accurately model it until two-thirds of the way through the ACTIVE program. To model the nozzle accurately, researchers had to be able to isolate and measure its movement and effects. In contrast to the X-31 and F-16 MATV testbeds, which relied on "inner-loop" control laws that automatically integrated thrust-vectoring into the aircraft's main control system, F-15 ACTIVE researchers wanted to conduct a good portion of their experiments in an "outer-loop" configuration that could isolate and gather data on specific nozzle movements and positions.[7]

By 1992, Pratt & Whitney had successfully fabricated, assembled, and ground tested a Pitch/Yaw Balanced Beam Nozzle (P/Y BBN) for its F100-PW-229 engine (rated for 29,000 pounds of thrust). Two years later, the ACTIVE research program was formalized to test Pratt & Whitney's design in flight. The ACTIVE program partners were Pratt & Whitney, McDonnell Douglas, U.S. Air Force Wright Laboratories, and NASA. NASA had not been involved in the S/MTD program but, as with the X-31 program, Dryden's ability to absorb the cost of providing its facilities offered important indirect funding assistance. Dryden also had done a great deal of related work with integrated flight and propulsion controls, especially with its F-15 Highly Integrated Digital Electronic Controls (HIDEC) aircraft. In addition, the S/MTD research had taken place at Edwards so it was a project familiar to Dryden, and NASA hired the Air Force's S/MTD lead flight controls engineer, Gerard Schkolnik, to develop the ACTIVE program technical objectives. Many of the team members from the Air Force, P&W, and McDonnell Douglas who had worked together on the S/MTD effort led the ACTIVE program as well.

The two main objectives of the ACTIVE flight test program were to demonstrate the operability of the Pratt & Whitney nozzle, and to quantify the performance and safety benefits introduced by the addition of a multi-axis thrust-vectoring system. Along the way, four goals were set out. First, to evaluate Pratt & Whitney's nozzle throughout a gradually expanding envelope up to Mach 2 and up to 30 degrees angle of attack. Second, to investigate the interaction between the airframe and nozzles and evaluate the aerodynamic and structural effects of vectoring the engine thrust. Third, to conduct performance testing both with and without thrust-vectoring, as a means of quantifying the benefits of the airframe/nozzle system. The final objective was to test and evaluate the AdAPT sensors and software on the aircraft.

Air Force officials agreed to lend NASA the F-15 S/MTD aircraft for the ACTIVE research, and the aircraft arrived at Dryden on 15 June 1993. The S/MTD was a unique platform and well suited to a thrust-vectoring flight test project for several reasons. The aircraft was among the first pre-production F-15Bs, and had already been modified for the S/MTD program with a quadruplex digital flight and propulsion control system. No mechanical links remained in either system, giving the plane added flexibility for purposes of integrated system research. The aircraft also had been modified with glass cockpit displays and advanced hydraulic and electric systems, as well as forward canards (made of two F-18 stabilators) that would give the pilot additional control authority if necessary.[8]

[7] James Smolka, et. al, "ACTIVE F-15 Flight Research Program," SETP 40th Annual Symposium Proceedings, ISSN#0742-3705, (Beverly Hills, CA: September 1996), 112-117; Gerard Schkolnik and James Smolka, interviewed by the author, Edwards, CA, 8 May 2001; Joe Pahle, interviewed by the author, 16 August 2001; John S. Orme and Robert L. Sims, "Selected Performance Measurements of the F-15 ACTIVE Axisymmetric Thrust-Vectoring Nozzle," paper, presented at the 14th ISABE (International Society for Airbreathing Engines) Annual Symposium, IS 166, (Florence, Italy: 5-10 September 1999), 1-2; Gerard Schkolnik and Jim Smolka, "F-15 Advanced Control Technology for Integrated Vehicles," presentation to the Royal Aeronautical Society's 1999 Fighter Conference, 30 September 1999; "ACTIVE AdAPT Sensor Study Objectives and Requirements," document, 7 December 1993, DFRC Historical Reference Collection.

[8] Smolka, et. al, "ACTIVE F-15 Flight Research Program," 112-117; "F-15 Advanced Control Technology for Integrated Vehicles (ACTIVE) Project Plan," 12 April 1994, DFRC Historical Reference Collection; Don Gatlin, interviewed by the author, 14 August 2001.

Aircraft Modifications

The first two phases of the ACTIVE research, which took place in mid-1994, focused on functional check flights of the aircraft, pilot qualifications, and obtaining baseline data for performance measurements. These phases were flown using non-vectoring F100-PW-100 engines and flight control laws that had been used in the S/MTD program.

At the conclusion of Phase 1 flights (the functional check flights were designated Phase 0), the aircraft underwent extensive modifications to prepare it for the thrust-vectoring phases of the program. The F100-PW-100 engines were replaced with the greater-thrust F100-PW-229 engines with the P/YBBN, a modification that also required reinforcing the airplane's aft-end structure to enable it to withstand up to 4,000 lbf (pounds of force) in yawing forces created by the thrust-vectoring nozzles. The aircraft structure had been modified for the S/MTD program to withstand pitch-vectoring loads of up to 6,000 foot-pounds. But no wind tunnel data was available for the ACTIVE configuration, so researchers opted to adhere to very conservative limits. On-board load and rate-limiting software limited the vector loads to 4,000 lbf in any direction. Even though the nozzles were capable of deflecting up to 20 degrees off centerline, if the 4,000 lbf-load limit was reached before a 20-degree deflection was achieved, the limiters would prevent further nozzle deflection.

Concern about over-stressing the aircraft with vector loads was greater in the F-15 ACTIVE than in other thrust-vectoring research programs for two reasons. First, other programs had relied on airframe-mounted paddles to vector the thrust. The ACTIVE thrust-vectoring system was incorporated into the engine; the engine mounts, which would have to absorb the vector loads, were not strengthened because the team wanted to maintain interoperability with fleet aircraft. Second, the ACTIVE test plan called for evaluating the thrust-vectoring system over a wider flight envelope than had been attempted in other programs. Vectoring the thrust of the F-15 at lower altitudes (20,000 feet) and up to Mach 2 would put more strain on the F-15 airframe than experimental thrust-vectoring systems had imposed on the airframes of the subsonic F-18 HARV or F-16 MATV. This also

meant that an extensive amount of simulation was used in the research effort to insure that maneuvers called for in the flight test plan wouldn't create problems. A high-fidelity, hardware-in-the-loop simulation was conducted in Dryden's Integrated Test Facility (ITF) and in simulators at McDonnell Douglas in St. Louis, and all test points were evaluated in the ITF simulator before flight.[9]

In addition to engine modifications, numerous computerized flight and engine controllers were added to the F-15 testbed to allow evaluation of individual components and optimal integration of all the aircraft's potential control effectors (aerodynamic and propulsion). Improved digital electronic engine, air inlet, and nozzle controllers were installed, as was an advanced Vehicle Management System Computer (VMSC) to perform the intensive calculations necessary for the real-time performance-enhancing algorithms researchers sought to test. The VMSC also integrated all the various aerodynamic and propulsion controllers. All told, the F-15 ACTIVE flight control system incorporated 10 computers (two nozzle controllers, two inlet controllers, two engine controllers, two flight control computers, the VMSC, and the aircraft's central computer). Separation of the engine controller from the nozzle controller added an extra degree of safety, as the separation allowed full engine capability even in the event of thrust-vectoring system failure.

The aircraft also was equipped with numerous sensors and extensive instrumentation. Strain gages were installed on the left engine mounts to measure the forces imposed by vectoring the engine thrust. A variety of pressure and temperature sensors also were added to the left engine nozzle, and one of the nozzle's divergent flaps was instrumented with static pressure transducers. This instrumentation allowed researchers to perform detailed pressure and temperature surveys of the nozzle during vectoring. Through the extensive instrumentation installed on the F-15 ACTIVE, a total of 3,377 parameters were recorded on board and

[9] "Advanced Control Technology For Integrated Vehicles (ACTIVE) Phase 2B Flight Test Plan," NASA Dryden Flight Research Center document, 24 June 1997, 58, DFRC Historical Reference Collection; Larry Walker, et. al, "ACTIVE F-15 Flight Research Program," presentation notes from the SETP 40th Annual Symposium Proceedings, (Beverly Hills, CA: September 1996), section 4, 2 and 11, from Gerard Schkolnik personal files.

The ACTIVE F-15 in flight over California's Antelope Valley, near Edwards Air Force Base. The type of exhaust nozzle on the aircraft was dubbed the "pitch/yaw balanced beam nozzle;" it allowed axisymmetric thrust-vectoring up to 20 degrees in any direction.

telemetered to the NASA control room during flight tests.[10]

Ground tests of the modified aircraft began in June 1995. The aircraft was first tested to verify that it could withstand the structural loads of a thrust-vectoring system. These "cold loads" tests were conducted using hydraulic rams to generate the test loads. The engines were then installed in the airframe for a second round of "hot loads" ground tests. These verified the structural integrity of the airframe and engine mounts and further calibrated the instrumentation attached to the engine. Additional ground tests included ground-vibration tests, hardware-in-the-loop simulation testing of the inte-

grated flight control and nozzle system, and a complete combined systems test on a ground thrust stand. Finally, in February 1996, the modified F-15 ACTIVE Flight Research Facility was ready.[11] The first flight took place on 14 February 1996, and on 27 March 1996, the plane completed its first thrust-vectoring flight.

Phase II Flight Test

ACTIVE thrust-vectoring research was divided into two primary phases. In the first, the central goal was to validate and gather data on the performance

[10] Larry Walker, et. al, "ACTIVE F-15 Flight Research Program," presentation notes; Orme and Sims, "Selected Performance Measurements of the F-15 ACTIVE Axisymmetric Thrust-Vectoring Nozzle," 2-4; Doane, et. al, "F-15 ACTIVE: A Flexible Propulsion Integration Testbed," 2-4; "F-15 Advanced Control Technology for Integrated Vehicles (ACTIVE) Project Plan," 4-7; Smolka, et. al, "ACTIVE F-15 Flight Research Program," 115-126.

[11] "F-15 Advanced Control Technology for Integrated Vehicles (ACTIVE) Project Plan"; Orme and Sims, "Selected Performance Measurements of the F-15 ACTIVE Axisymmetric Thrust-Vectoring Nozzle," 2-4; Bruce Wood, interviewed by the author, 24 April 2002; Doane, et. al, "F-15 ACTIVE: A Flexible Propulsion Integration Testbed," 4-5; J.D. Hunley, "NASA Tests New Nozzle to Improve Performance," *The X-Press*, Vol. 38, Issue 4, April 1996, 1.

and effects of the thrust-vectoring system throughout the F-15 flight envelope. So the F-15 ACTIVE was used to create a kind of "wind tunnel in the sky" for propulsion research, much as the F-18 HARV had done in the field of aerodynamics research. Instead of using thrust-vectoring as an integral part of the aircraft's flight control system, the researchers stored pre-programmed thrust-vectoring commands and maneuvers into the VMSC. The pilot would stabilize the aircraft at a given condition, relying on the right-hand engine for stability and control. He would then select one of 15 datasets preprogrammed to command the thrust-vectoring deflections to be performed by the left-hand engine, which had the bulk of the instrumentation, and the aircraft would automatically perform the commanded function. These automated, isolated maneuvers, much like those commanded by the F-18 HARV On-Board Excitation System, allowed researchers to get specific, isolated, and repeatable data points on the pressures and loads created by thrust-vectoring angles and conditions. Data was recorded during both steady-state conditions and more dynamic maneuvers, with the pilot making large throttle movements.

All of these empirical data points helped researchers characterize, model, and understand the behavior and dynamics of the Pratt & Whitney thrust-vectoring nozzle and system. This understanding was important for two reasons. The first was that one of the significant challenges in designing a production-quality thrust-vectoring nozzle for a fighter was insuring that the thrust-vectoring system wouldn't create greater forces, or loads, on the aircraft than the aircraft could withstand at any point in the flight envelope. Without a thorough understanding of the actual loads in different flight conditions, the only way to insure this was to build in a substantial safety margin that limited the impact the thrust-vectoring system could have on the aircraft. While this would resolve the safety issue, it also would limit the potential benefits of incorporating thrust-vectoring into an aircraft.

A second challenge in designing a production-quality thrust-vectoring system was designing control laws that would give the pilot the amount of vectoring force necessary to accomplish the commanded maneuver. Being able to supply the correct amount of vectoring without a lot of adjustment within the control system was important in order to give thrust-vectored aircraft

good handling characteristics and responsiveness. And it would be essential for any future design that relied on the technology for flight-critical stability and control functions.

To resolve these issues, researchers needed to know how much force the thrust-vectoring system actually generated at different conditions. This was very difficult, because determining the vector force required measuring the amount of thrust an engine was creating, and researchers had no good way of measuring actual thrust in flight. Existing thrust-measurement systems relied on processing flight data after the fact to extract approximate thrust values. And so, among the ACTIVE program's big successes was the development of a more accurate approach to measuring real-time engine thrust in flight. The system developed for the ACTIVE flight tests used strain gages installed on the aircraft's left engine mounts to determine the forces generated by the engine in both non-vectored and vectored flight. The gages were carefully calibrated during a full year of ground testing, and then adjustments were made to compensate for aerodynamic flight forces such as g loads and airflow interactions. The result was a more accurate, direct measurement of the F-15 ACTIVE testbed's thrust. In addition to providing reassurance that vector loads were remaining within the airframe's structural limits, this real-time measurement of thrust was a critical step toward developing future flight-critical propulsion control systems.

The in-flight thrust measurements collected allowed researchers to determine the loads and vector forces being generated at a wide range of flight and nozzle conditions. Surprisingly, researchers found that the actual loads on the actuators controlling nozzle movement were significantly lower than had been predicted. This permitted increase of the minimum rate of nozzle deflection at high power and high speeds.[12]

The data obtained through this "open-loop" testing

---

[12] Timothy R. Conners and Robert L. Sims, "Full Flight Envelope Direct Thrust Measurement on a Supersonic Aircraft," NASA TM-1998-206560, July 1998, 1-6; Bruce Wood, interviewed by the author, 24 April, 2002; Ron Ray, interviewed by the author, 17 August 2001; Schkolnik and Smolka, interviewed by the author, 8 May 2001; Orme and Sims, "Selected Performance Measurements of the F-15 ACTIVE Axisymmetric Thrust-Vectoring Nozzle," 4-10; "Advanced Control Technology For Integrated Vehicles (ACTIVE) Phase 2B Flight Test Plan," 24; Schkolnik, interviewed by the author, 25 April 2002.

also gave ACTIVE researchers the confidence to expand the aircraft's flight test envelope into the supersonic range within four weeks of the first thrust-vectoring flight. On 24 April 1996, the aircraft demonstrated thrust-vectoring at Mach 1.5 at an altitude of 40,000 feet–a flight witnessed by a large media contingent on the ground. Six months later, the F-15 ACTIVE successfully demonstrated thrust-vectoring at a speed of almost Mach 2–the fastest multi-axis thrust-vectoring ever achieved with any aircraft.[13]

The open-loop flight experiments also gave researchers valuable data about the effectiveness of the P/Y BBN thrust-vectoring nozzle. Data was collected at three power settings: cruise, military power, and maximum power. One interesting result was that researchers found the overall thrust efficiency of the engine to be greater when the nozzle was vectored slightly downward than when it was in a straight, non-vectored position. In addition, while researchers' predictions about vector force were fairly accurate at lower-power settings, the nozzle generated significantly less vector force than predicted at maximum-power settings. The nozzle also was less effective at supersonic speeds than it was at subsonic speeds. This data allowed researchers to refine and modify the on-board models of the P/Y BBN and the aircraft's control laws to allow for greater and more accurate nozzle-vectoring angles before the program moved on to the next phase of inner-loop flight testing.[14]

Throughout Phase 2 of the F-15 ACTIVE flight tests, the only significant mechanical problem researchers encountered was that at higher speeds the nozzle's individual flaps and seals tended to bind and catch on each other, causing some bending damage to the nozzle feathers. The problem may have been caused at least in part by the honeycomb composite structure used for the nozzle feathers in an attempt to minimize system weight. As the nozzle gyrated at high speeds, the seals between the nozzle feathers may have caught on the sharp edges of the honeycomb skin. Adjustments were made to the flap and seal configuration to improve the problem before the inner-loop phase of flight tests, which incorporated the thrust-vectoring system into the central flight control system of the aircraft. The issue was not entirely resolved, but Pratt & Whitney engineers considered the difficulty something that could be fixed fairly easily in a next-generation nozzle design, and they pointed to its discovery as one of the valuable benefits resulting from the F-15 ACTIVE program.[15]

High Stability Engine Control (HISTEC)

In addition to the basic nozzle verification, envelope expansion, and vector-force modeling, several other research projects were conducted with the aircraft during Phase II of the ACTIVE program. One of these focused on an intelligent engine control concept called High Stability Engine Control (HISTEC), in a research effort managed at NASA's Lewis Research Center but tested on the ACTIVE aircraft at Dryden. The impetus for the HISTEC program was the realization on the part of designers and researchers that as fighter aircraft moved further into unusual attitudes and low-observability designs, the likelihood increased that disturbed airflows through the engine inlets would be a recurring problem. Designers could compensate for this distortion by simply designing engines with large stall margins, allowing even disturbed flows to generate enough airflow to keep the engine running. But such margins degraded potential engine performance. HISTEC research involved an intelligent engine-control concept designed to continually measure the distortion of the inlet airflow in flight and adjust the engine performance (stall margin) accordingly so that an optimal amount of stall margin was maintained.

NASA had previously tested similar integrated control concepts to provide real-time compensation for inlet distortion with its HIDEC program, flight research that

[13] Bruce A. Smith, "F-15 ACTIVE Tests Supersonic Yaw Vectoring, *Aviation Week & Space Technology*, 29 April, 1996, reprint, DFRC Historical Reference Collection; Alan Brown, "F-15 Thrusts to Almost Mach 2," *The Dryden X-Press*, 6 December 1996, 1, 3; Doane, interviewed by the author, 29 April 2002.

[14] Wood, interviewed by the author, 24 April, 2002; Schkolnik and Smolka, "F-15 Advanced Control Technology for Integrated Vehicles," 9; Larry Walker, et. al, "ACTIVE F-15 Flight Research Program"; Orme and Sims, "Selected Performance Measurements of the F-15 ACTIVE Axisymmetric Thrust-Vectoring Nozzle," 4-10.

[15] Wood, interviewed by the author, 24 April, 2002; Orme and Sims, "Selected Performance Measurements of the F-15 ACTIVE Axisymmetric Thrust-Vectoring Nozzle," 6; Larry Walker, et. al, "ACTIVE F-15 Flight Research Program," 6; Bursey, interviewed by the author, 26 April 2002.

also utilized an F-15 testbed. What made the HISTEC program different was that it offered a better and more accurate technique for estimating inlet distortion and its effect on engine stability. HISTEC research entailed use of a series of high-response static pressure sensors at the engine face, after which data was processed through a new algorithm to determine correct engine response to airflow conditions.

Flight-testing the HISTEC program software did not require an aircraft with thrust-vectoring capability. In fact, the entire series of HISTEC research flights was conducted without engaging the F-15 ACTIVE testbed's thrust-vectoring system. But the advanced and integrated digital electronic inlet and engine controllers on the F-15 *were* important for the flight tests, making the F-15 an excellent testbed on which to explore the concept. The HISTEC experiments were conducted with the right-hand engine of the airplane, as opposed to the open-loop ACTIVE research conducted primarily with the left-hand engine. Additional instrumentation was installed in the right-hand engine inlet. Another computer was added to process data collected with the right-hand engine instrumentation in real time and generate the appropriate engine control commands. The computer also incorporated data from the aircraft's flight control system to predict impending inlet distortions.

The HISTEC flight research was conducted in two phases. The first was an open-loop verification of the algorithm and distortion database. Next, in a series of closed-loop experiments, the HISTEC software controlled engine fan and compressor response to different inlet distortion conditions. A total of 10 flights were made with the system during the summer of 1997, testing conditions up to an angle of attack of 29 degrees and speeds up to Mach 1.5. The results were impressive. Very few adjustments to the estimation algorithm were needed, and the system efficiently applied stability-enhancing engine trim to compensate for high levels of inlet distortion. Even in conditions where significant inlet distortion occurred, the F-15

ACTIVE aircraft experienced no engine stalls during HISTEC research. The HISTEC algorithm also required so few adjustments that the research effort was completed in six weeks instead of the three months that was forecast.[16]

Adaptive Aircraft Performance Technology (AdAPT)

A second algorithm concept, called Adaptive Aircraft Performance Technology (AdAPT), also was tested during Phase II of the ACTIVE program. While the HISTEC algorithm and software focused on optimizing engine performance for different flight and inlet distortion conditions, the AdAPT algorithm aimed to optimize the trim settings of all the aircraft control effectors to produce better range or excess power. The F-15 ACTIVE testbed had 14 potential control effectors; combinations of seven, including use of collective stabilator, canard, collective aileron, inlet ramp position, nozzle area ratio, collective pitch vectoring, and differential yaw vectoring, were examined in the AdAPT program.

The AdAPT research quantified the reaction of individual control effectors to excitation and the excitation's effect on aircraft performance. From those results, the AdAPT algorithm produced a set of optimal trim settings for different flight conditions. Those results, then, were sent to the aircraft's flight controller. Tests were done in two modes, one that limited the acceleration and pitch rate of the optimization (generating a smoother ride for the pilot) and one that did not.

The AdAPT flight tests showed that optimizing trim settings would improve aircraft cruise performance. In one flight experiment, the F-15's cruise speed was increased from Mach 1.2 to Mach 1.3 after the AdAPT system optimized the aircraft's trim settings. The results verified the AdAPT algorithm and illustrated that it was possible for an adaptive controller to calculate optimal combinations of control effectors in flight for either better efficiency or excess power, making the technology useful for both future commercial and military aircraft applications. In fact, the technology developed through the ACTIVE program was later patented, and derivatives of it were incorporated into the Intelligent Flight Control System program.[17]

[16] Robert D. Southwick, "High Stability Engine Control (HISTEC): Phase IIIB Final Report," NASA/CR-1999-209315, August 1999, 1-4, 56-59; John S. Orme, et. al, "Development and Testing of a High Stability Engine Control (HISTEC) System," NASA/TM-1998-206562, July 1998, 1-13; John Orme, interviewed by the author, 29 April 2002.

Intelligent Flight Control System (IFCS)

The idea of adaptive performance optimization was taken a step further in the IFCS research phase of the ACTIVE program. Dryden researchers already had done quite a bit of work on integrated propulsion and flight controls with the HIDEC F-15 testbed, ranging from digital electronic engine control and performance seeking engine control research to experiments exploring the possibility of controlling an aircraft solely with the use of its propulsion system.

In 1989-1990, Dryden and the Air Force had conducted a Self-Repairing Flight Control System (SRFCS) flight-test program with the HIDEC F-15. SRFCS research focused on the ability of an integrated propulsion and flight control system to identify battle damage to an aircraft's control surfaces and compensate for the degradation in control authority by using other flight controls, including the aircraft's engines. An IFCS was a more sophisticated and robust approach to the same problem. With an intelligent flight control system, an "intelligent," neural network of sensors would continually measure the aircraft's stability and control parameters in flight. The system would then calculate any deficiencies and optimize a combination of all other control effectors to compensate for damage or failure. Unlike the SRFCS, which focused on the loss of individual control surfaces, an IFCS could compensate for a variety of problems, including loss of structural components or other internal system failures.

ACTIVE IFCS flight tests were conducted in a mode in which control would revert to the standard F-15 control laws and configuration if a fault were detected. This allowed a more rapid envelope expansion. The IFCS was tested at various points throughout the F-15 envelope, from subsonic through supersonic flight, and for completion of precision tasks such as close formation and air-to-air tracking; the test pilots who evaluated the system gave it very high marks for generating good handling characteristics in flight.

The IFCS experiments conducted with the F-15 ACTIVE were only a first step in intelligent flight controls research. The system tested on the ACTIVE testbed was a pre-trained and fixed one, and therefore not a true adaptive system. But the ACTIVE IFCS flights proved that a pre-trained neural network could be the foundation for a future real-time, adaptive flight control system. More development was needed to make such a system operational. The IFCS flight experiments with the F-15 ACTIVE showed enough promise that further research on the concept continued at Dryden even after the conclusion of the F-15 ACTIVE program. In addition to expanding the research to online learning networks, the follow-on effort, involving not only the F-15 but also a C-17 transport, focused on development of a system sufficiently adaptable and generic that it would be interchangeable among aircraft.[18]

Range Extension and High Speed Acoustic Research

Another performance evaluation conducted during Phase II of the ACTIVE flight research was a demonstration of how thrust-vectoring and the Pratt & Whitney P/Y BBN design might potentially extend the range of the Air Force F-15E. The control settings of the F-15 ACTIVE were adjusted to compensate for the ACTIVE aircraft's forward canard, which the F-15E did not have. With that adjustment made, researchers experimented with both pitch vectoring and adjustment of the nozzle's area ratio to determine whether drag could be reduced enough to extend an F-15's range. The results were impressive, showing a 4.1 percent drag reduction over the aircraft's entire flight envelope, which translated into a 4.3 percent combat radius for the F-15E Strike Eagle.

[17] Doane, et. al, "F-15 ACTIVE: A Flexible Propulsion Integration Testbed," 6-7; "Advanced Control Technology For Integrated Vehicles (ACTIVE) Phase 2B Flight Test Plan," 35; Schkolnik, interviewed by the author, 25 April 2002; M. Hreha, et. al, "An Approach to Aircraft Performance Optimization Using Thrust-vectoring," AIAA paper 94-3361, presented at the 30th AIAA/ASMESAE/ASEE Joint Propulsion Conference (Indianapolis, IN: 27-29 June 1994), 1-2, 8-11; "Propulsion and Performance Branch 1993-1994 Biennial Report," DFRC Historical Reference Collection.

[18] Schkolnik and Smolka, "F-15 Advanced Control Technology for Integrated Vehicles," 17-19; Doane, et. al, "F-15 ACTIVE: A Flexible Propulsion Integration Testbed," 7; Gerard S. Schkolnik, "Integrated Control Systems for Aircraft and Turbine Engines, Research Status, Performance Seeking Controls, Flight Test Programs," presentation viewgraphs, UTSI Aero-Propulsion Systems Technology, Test and Evaluation Short Course, 16 April 1997, DFRC Historical Reference Collection; Frank W. Burcham, interviewed by the author, Edwards, CA, 24 August 1995; Schkolnik, interviewed by the author, 25 April 2002; Orme, interviewed by the author, 29 April 2002.

ACTIVE researchers also conducted a series of experiments with the variable area-ratio capability of the Pratt & Whitney nozzle for the High Speed Civil Transport (HSCT) program. The HSCT program was cancelled, but at the time ACTIVE experiments were being conducted one of the driving design concerns of the HSCT focused on the acoustics levels of a supersonic jet. That noise level was, in part, a function of the sharp change in pressure that occurs when high-speed, low-pressure engine exhaust collides with ambient air behind the exhaust nozzle. Because the area ratio of an F-15 ACTIVE testbed's engine nozzles was adjustable, allowing the exhaust pressure to be changed, researchers were able to evaluate different area ratios and engine settings affecting the noise generated by the engine. To evaluate the impact of these changes on the aircraft's noise signature, the F-15 was flown over arrays of microphones that measured noise levels at different nozzle and engine settings. These experiments collected data over a wide range of flight conditions that researchers could then use to refine and improve their design tools.[19]

Phase III Flight Research

Phase II of the ACTIVE research program consisted of open-loop research, in which the thrust-vectoring capability of the F-15 aircraft was turned on and off by the pilot during controlled experiments but was not incorporated as an integral part of the aircraft's basic flight control software. By isolating different thrust-vectoring settings and movements, researchers were better able to characterize the vector loads, performance, and efficiency of the Pratt & Whitney nozzle and system. The next step was to integrate thrust-vectoring capability into the plane's basic flight control system, using the more accurate thrust-vectoring system models generated by the Phase II experiments. This inner-loop thrust-vectoring was the primary focus of the F-15 ACTIVE Phase III flight

research, though the project actually had two main goals.

The first was to validate the modified vector efficiency and nozzle models that had been developed using data from Phase II. But researchers also sought to evaluate the flying qualities of the aircraft using thrust-vectoring as a primary method of flight control. The flight control hardware and software of the F-15 ACTIVE testbed had been designed to permit a wide range of options, from thrust-vectoring only to aerodynamic control only, and to incorporate various combinations of control effectors. The flight control laws used for the Phase III research, developed jointly by NASA and McDonnell Douglas, were designed to use thrust-vectoring to the maximum extent possible. The control laws then augmented the thrust-vectoring control as necessary with aerodynamic controls. This was a dramatically different approach from that taken in other thrust-vectoring research, in which the propulsion and aerodynamic controls had been combined more evenly in attempts to optimize aircraft performance and handling.

ACTIVE researchers took a different approach for two reasons. First, the ACTIVE program came on the heels of the other three research efforts. Thus the basic feasibility of multi-axis thrust-vectoring, and the ability of thrust-vectoring to offer good handling characteristics when combined with the aircraft's aerodynamic controls, had already been demonstrated. So the ACTIVE team wanted to take a slightly different approach in the hope of getting a clearer picture of the effectiveness, handling characteristics, and capabilities of multi-axis thrust-vectoring by using it as a primary control effector. Second, ACTIVE researchers sought to evaluate the use of thrust-vectoring to replace aerodynamic controls altogether. In fact, several Phase III research flights were conducted with the aerodynamic pitch controls turned off, so that pitch control was entirely dependent on the thrust-vectoring system.

The inner-loop flight tests began in November 1998. Pilots were given tasks representative of those a fighter pilot would have to accomplish, such as close-formation flying and air-to-air tracking. Surprisingly, pilots rated the handling characteristics of the thrust-vectoring-dependent control laws more highly than they had the standard control laws that relied on standard aerodynamic controls. Even flights with aerodynamic

---

[19] "Advanced Control Technology For Integrated Vehicles (ACTIVE) Phase 2B Flight Test Plan," 27; Schkolnik, interviewed by the author, 25 April 2002; Bursey, interviewed by the author, 26 April 2002; Doane, et. al, "F-15 ACTIVE: A Flexible Propulsion Integration Testbed," 6; Bruce A. Smith, "F-15 ACTIVE Tests Supersonic Yaw Vectoring," *Aviation Week & Space Technology*.

pitch controls turned off received high satisfaction ratings from the pilots. In addition to validating the control laws used for Phase III flights, the pilots' ratings verified the accuracy of the revised models for the nozzle's effectiveness at different flight conditions; had the models been inaccurate, the aircraft's responsiveness would not have scored high marks. Perhaps even more important, the pilots' favorable ratings validated the feasibility of using only thrust-vectoring to control an aircraft, at least in pitch.

After receiving positive ratings from pilots on propulsion pitch control of the aircraft in flight, ACTIVE researchers wanted to proceed with a demonstration of a full landing in the aircraft using only thrust-vectoring to control the F-15's pitch. The idea of landing an aircraft using only propulsion for control was not new. In 1993, Dryden research pilot C. Gordon Fullerton had demonstrated a successful landing in an F-15 using only differential engine power for control of the aircraft–in all axes–as part of NASA's Propulsion Controlled Aircraft (PCA) research. But thrust-vectoring offered even more flexibility for control than did PCA technology. Indeed, Navy officials took the X-31 out of storage to pursue the VECTOR Extremely Short Take Off and Landing (ESTOL) research program in 2000 because they recognized the potential thrust-vectoring offered in terms of landing performance. But with the F-15 ACTIVE testbed, use of propulsion control of pitch all the way through landing was never actually demonstrated because the program ended before the experiment could be carried out.[20]

MANX and MANTA

The prevailing approach to thrust-vectoring, in research ranging from the S/MTD and the F-22 programs to those of the X-31 and the F-15 ACTIVE, was to design an aircraft that could fly without thrust-vectoring and then add two- or three-dimensional vectoring to create additional capabilities or benefits. The X-31's quasi-tailless experiments, however, fueled a growing recognition among researchers that some of thrust-vectoring's most significant benefits might come through using it to open the door on an entirely new realm of aircraft design. Use of thrust-vectoring to supplement or replace some of the aerodynamic stability and control

functions of aircraft components or control surfaces, they realized, might allow some conventional aerodynamic surfaces to be reduced or eliminated altogether.

The hesitancy among designers and pilots to leave so much riding on the integrity and performance of an engine was substantial. In part, the hesitancy stemmed from realistic concerns about reliability; if an F-16 fighter jet's single engine fails, the pilot generally has either enough altitude or enough airspeed to attempt a restart or ejection before the airplane goes out of control. If the engine were to flame out or fail in an aircraft whose design relied on the propulsion system for critical stability and control, the consequences would be much more immediate and severe–which made the concept all the more challenging. The McDonnell Douglas candidate for the Joint Strike Fighter competition featured a tailless design that was dependent on thrust-vectoring for control in portions of its high-alpha flight envelope. Even though the design did not require thrust-vectoring for basic stability and control throughout most of its flight regime, the U.S. Navy balked at specifying thrust-vectoring as a flight-critical component in any portion of the flight envelope.

Nevertheless, the ACTIVE research had made all its team members strong believers in the benefits that thrust-vectoring could offer if it could be incorporated in a more central way into an aircraft design. They saw that the technology could significantly reduce aircraft drag, radar cross-section, and weight, and increase range and fuel capacity. Thrust-vectoring capability could also render aircraft more maneuverable. So, as the formal ACTIVE program was winding down in the late 1990s, both McDonnell Douglas and NASA engineers began pushing for different follow-on projects that would allow them to take use of the technology to the next step.

The design favored by McDonnell Douglas engineers was a highly modified, tailless F-15 design called Manx, after the tailless cat from the Isle of Man.[21]

[20] Schkolnik and Smolka, "F-15 Advanced Control Technology for Integrated Vehicles," 13-16; Schkolnik, interviewed by the author, 25 April 2002; Bursey, interviewed by the author, 26 April 2002; Ramon Lopez, "ACTIVE Takes Step To Propulsion Control," *Flight International*, 23 December 1998 – 5 January 1999, 13.

[22] See previous discussion in Chapter One, footnote no. 21.[21] The name MANX actually stood for Multi-Axis vectoring No-tail eXperiment, but the acronym was a tortuous attempt to allow the project to be called Manx, after the tailless cat.

McDonnell Douglas conducted feasibility studies on the design and even performed wind tunnel testing of a model in England in the late 1990s. These tests indicated that the design would be directionally and longitudinally as unstable as the X-29, but that the concept was feasible. The feasibility studies also indicated that the program could be flight tested for as little as $12 million, since engineers proposed to use the already well-documented and thrust-vectoring-equipped F-15 ACTIVE aircraft for the tests. Support for the program never materialized, however, and the effort didn't proceed beyond wind tunnel testing.

At the same time, NASA researchers were advocating an even more radical follow-on program–a propulsion-dependent design called the X-44A Multi Axis No Tail Aircraft (MANTA). While not a "clean sheet" design, the MANTA proposal called for taking one of the prototype F-22 aircraft and modifying it to eliminate not only its horizontal and vertical tail surfaces, but also all of its aerodynamic flight control surfaces: all functions performed by those surfaces would be performed by two multi-axis thrust-vectoring engines.

It was a radical notion and would have been expensive to pursue. NASA researchers estimated that the effort would have cost somewhere between $200 and $400 million–akin to the $300 million that the Air Force S/MTD program reportedly cost, but still an expensive endeavor. The team actually did obtain funding for a one-year feasibility study on the project with Lockheed-Martin and Pratt & Whitney, and the study indicated a MANTA-type design potentially held significant benefits. But priorities in the military and in NASA's aeronautical research were changing, and budgets were shrinking. The concept also may have involved too radical a paradigm shift in aircraft design to win the support it needed. In any event, the X-44A MANTA never proceeded beyond the feasibility-study stage.

At the same time, funding and support for other propulsion control research experiments the F-15 ACTIVE team had hoped to pursue were also drying up. ACTIVE researchers had wanted to conduct further experiments using only thrust-vectoring for primary flight control functions, but the program was closed down after its propulsion-dependent pitch control

flight experiments. The aircraft, whose ownership had been signed over to Dryden partway through the ACTIVE research program, remained at Dryden for follow-on IFCS experiments. But by the fall of 1999, the formal F-15 ACTIVE program had come to an end.[22]

Conclusion

The F-15 ACTIVE program set out two basic goals. The first was to verify, model, and evaluate Pratt & Whitney's P/Y BBN thrust-vectoring nozzle in flight. The second was to take the detailed engine data from the first set of experiments and integrate them into a closed-loop propulsion and flight control system that would maximize the use of thrust-vectoring and evaluate its potential for efficiency and for aircraft control. ACTIVE research accomplished those goals, but also expanded into other experiments because the F-15's unique computers and integrated control systems made it an ideal testbed for several other research efforts as well. The HISTEC, AdAPT, IFCS, and HSCT acoustics research projects all were drawn to the ACTIVE platform because of its unique configuration and flexible research capabilities.

The ACTIVE research effort differed from the thrust-vectoring flight research programs that preceded it in two significant ways. First, its goal was to understand the specific dynamics and effectiveness of thrust-vectoring technology rather than to focus on the tactical or research benefits the technology could offer. Second, the ACTIVE program focused not on the high-angle-of-attack, low-speed range of flight but on higher-speed, lower-angle-of-attack portions of the flight envelope, where there was less confidence in the technology's effectiveness. The F-18 HARV, the X-31, and the F-16 MATV projects all examined thrust-vectoring's role in expanding a fighter's envelope at the low-speed, high-alpha edge of performance. The F-15

[22] Schkolnik, interviewed by the author, 30 March 2001; Nick Cook, "NASA Looks To New X-44A For Tail-less Experimental Research," *Janes Defense Weekly*, 6 October 1999, 5; Sean Kearns, "Experimental Aircraft May Be On Horizon," *Antelope Valley Press*, 11 July 1999, A-1, A-8; Schkolnik and Smolka, interviewed by the author, 8 May 2001; Denis Bessette, interviewed by the author, 10 August 2001; Doane, interviewed by the author, 29 April, 2002; Orme, interviewed by the author, 29 April, 2002.

ACTIVE program, by contrast, examined exclusively the benefits thrust-vectoring could offer within the rest of a fighter's existing flight envelope.

Yet even though the research was conducted within the normal flight envelope, the fact that the design of the Pratt & Whitney nozzle was an experimental one and that researchers hadn't identified the precise loads that would be imposed on the aircraft by thrust-vectoring at high power and high speeds made the research challenging to execute. NASA, McDonnell Douglas, and Pratt & Whitney engineers spent as much time updating and integrating the engine controls as they did the flight controls, to ensure that the system was in harmony. Fortunately, good working relationships existed among the partners–relationships bolstered by the fact that at least three of the project's principal managers had worked together on the Air Force S/MTD aircraft (the plane that became the ACTIVE research platform) prior to beginning work on the ACTIVE program.

Because the loads and stresses the vectoring system would put on the aircraft in flight were unknown, a great deal of emphasis was put on simulation and evaluation of test points before proceeding to flight. Even so, researchers found themselves surprised by in-flight results that did not match the simulation predictions. Fortunately, the simulation models had been conservative, but the discrepancy served as a reminder to the ACTIVE team that simulated results are not always a guarantee of what will be discovered in flight. That is, of course, why flight remains a critical component of aeronautical research. At the same time, it also was a cautionary reminder against becoming complacent about the safety of flight maneuvers using only simulation results as a barometer.[3]

There were some mechanical difficulties with Pratt & Whitney's nozzle flaps. Overall, however, the F-15 ACTIVE flight tests were very successful. Researchers validated a real-time, direct-thrust measurement system that could be used to aid any future propulsion-research effort aimed at identifying the loads and performance of an engine in flight. In addition, the program generated a tremendous amount of detailed data on the PW-F100-229 engine as well as on the vectoring nozzle that allowed Pratt & Whitney to verify and improve their computational fluid dynamics engine models. The flight tests also verified the potential benefits in both noise and drag reduction of the adjustable synchronization ring that the P/Y BBN nozzle incorporated–a feature that could be applied to new Pratt & Whitney engine designs.

Although the primary goal of the F-15 ACTIVE flight tests was to understand the dynamics of thrust-vectoring, the program also successfully demonstrated that the technology could, indeed, offer performance and efficiency benefits even within a fighter jet's normal flight envelope, at speeds up to Mach 2. In addition, the HISTEC, AdAPT, and IFCS research all illustrated the feasibility of intelligent systems that could make real-time, in-flight measurements and process that data through optimization algorithms, opening an entirely new realm of capabilities in terms of aircraft performance and safety.

But for all that was discovered and demonstrated through F-15 ACTIVE research about thrust-vectoring with an axisymmetric nozzle, it was becoming increasingly evident that mere improvements in efficiency or even maneuverability might not be enough for thrust-vectoring to "buy its way onto" a fighter plane. The technology also offered the potential for revolutionizing aircraft design by enabling tailless or other highly modified aircraft configurations. Taking advantage of that capability required use of thrust-vectoring for flight-critical stability and control functions. Researchers differed on how far such a design should go, and on how much the design should rely on a propulsion-based flight control system, but it was clear that any advances in this unproven and high-risk area would need to be developed and proven in flight before gaining any level of acceptance. Unfortunately, sufficient support for that kind of follow-on flight research did not exist when the F-15 ACTIVE program ended.

Nevertheless, the program's initial goals had been accomplished. Researchers had developed important tools and collected data that would be useful to any follow-on effort. Though engineers had been unable to explore thrust-vectoring technology to the extent they might have liked, they had expanded the existing knowledge base and paved the way for those who would follow them.

[23] Larry Walker, et. al, "ACTIVE F-15 Flight Research Program," section 4, 11.

Epilogue
A Proven Technology

The X-31, F-18 HARV, and F-15 ACTIVE research programs developed out of growing concern that fighter aircraft needed to be more maneuverable without risking loss of control. While the three programs had different goals, all were successful. Each advanced the body of knowledge about the dynamics and capabilities of thrust-vectoring technology. How that knowledge will be applied remains to be seen.

Researchers involved in all three thrust-vectoring programs saw the potential for the technology to do more than simply enhance existing fighter designs. With a mature thrust-vectoring system that could reliably control yaw and provide aircraft with directional stability, the basic design of high-performance aircraft could be revolutionized, perhaps even incorporating such radical changes as eliminating aerodynamic controls or vertical tails. Such changes would dramatically reduce aircraft drag. And because an aircraft's vertical tail is among the components most visible to enemy radar, this capability could also greatly enhance the low-observability of new fighter designs.

In the 1980s, researchers at Langley conducted a series of wind tunnel tests evaluating tailless versions of various high-performance aircraft models with thrust-vectoring capability, and these tests showed promise. In addition, there were plans in both the X-31 and the F-15 ACTIVE programs to test thrust-vectoring systems on tailless designs. The X-31 program contemplated future flight tests with the aircraft's tail reduced in size or removed altogether. NASA team members in the F-15 ACTIVE program had an even more ambitious plan. They hoped to flight test a tailless version of the F-22 Raptor using Pratt & Whitney's three-dimensional thrust-vectoring system for stability and control. Their proposed Multi-Axis No Tail Aircraft (MANTA) even received an X-Plane designation (X-44A), but funding for the project has yet to materialize.[1] Although neither of these purely tailless research efforts ever flew, some X-31 research flights were completed that simulated the behavior of a quasi-tailless X-31 aircraft through modifications of the plane's flight control computer system.

The X-31's quasi-tailless flight research was funded largely by the Department of Defense's Joint Advanced Strike Technology (JAST) program, which focused on potential technologies for the next generation Joint Strike Fighter (JSF) program. When the JSF final design was selected, however, it did not include either three-dimensional thrust-vectoring for maneuverability, a tailless or even a quasi-tailless design. The Short Take Off and Vertical Landing (STOVL) version of Lockheed-Martin's X-35 JSF design does include a certain amount of thrust-vectoring capability in its Pratt & Whitney JSF-119-611 engine (95 degrees downward from its horizontal position, and plus or minus 10 degrees laterally), but the goal of thrust-vectoring in this application was to give the aircraft extremely short takeoff and vertical landing performance rather than increased maneuverability in the air.[2]

If the F-18 HARV, X-31, F-16 MATV, and F-15 ACTIVE all helped illustrate the potential advantages of thrust-vectoring and advanced the development of both the hardware and software necessary to make the technology possible, why wasn't multi-axis thrust-vectoring incorporated into the JSF, or retrofitted into existing fighters for enhanced maneuverability? The reasons are varied, and illustrate the complexities of technology research and application.

---

[1] While funding for the X-44A aircraft has not materialized, the concept may still see the light of day. In the summer of 2002 Lockheed-Martin submitted an unsolicited proposal to the Air Force for an FB-22 deep strike fighter that bears an uncanny resemblance to the X-44A MANTA.

[2] Schkolnik, interviewed by author, 12 February 2001 and 30 March, 2001; Chambers, interviewed by author, 15 August, 2001; Smolka, interviewed by author, 17 August 2001; Denis Bessette, interviewed by author, 10 August 2001; Schkolnik and Smolka, "F-15 Advanced Control Technology for Integrated Vehicles; Chambers, *Partners in Freedom*, 193; B.F. Tamrat, et. al, "X-31 Quasi-Tailless Flight Test Experiment, Final Report," TFD-95-1261, draft, 9 June 1995, DFRC Historical Reference Collection; X-31 Flight Report 1-214, 10 March 1994, X-31 Flight Report 1-215, 10 March 1994, and X-31 Flight Report 1-216, 10 March 1994, DFRC Historical Reference Collection; "JAST Technology Maturation Utilizing the X-31 Testbed," briefing papers, VMS-BRF-95-06, DFRC Historical Reference Collection; "X-31/JAST FMIPT Meeting, briefing papers, 16 November 1994, DFRC Historical Reference Collection; Jennifer Young, X-31 Vector Program Manager, interviewed by author, 25 October 2001; Paul Lewis, "Lockheed-Martin: The Fort Worth Fighter," *Flight International*, supplement, 05-11 September 2000, 25-30; Guy Norris, "Thunder in the Desert," *Flight International*, supplement, 05-11 September 2000, 32-35; Peter Law, interviewed by author, 17 December 2001.

The military's support of multi-axis thrust-vectoring research was largely driven by a perceived need for aircraft that could maneuver better in a dogfight to gain "first-shot" firing capability with short-range missiles. But even while researchers were investigating and developing thrust-vectoring capability for aircraft, missile manufacturers were developing improved capabilities for short-range weapons. The latest generation of short-range missiles has superior maneuverability and tracking capabilities when compared to its predecessors, reducing the need for such enhanced maneuverability in the fighters launching the missiles. These advances, coupled with new helmet-mounted display technologies, seemed to offer the military many of the same tactical advantages that thrust-vectoring could, with lowered cost and complexity.

Concerns and questions about thrust-vectoring technology itself remained. Although the various research programs had shown that use of thrust-vectoring could offer impressive advantages over standard fighter designs, the capability also had potential drawbacks from a tactical viewpoint. A thrust-vectored fighter could turn on a dime and perform astounding high-alpha maneuvers, but those maneuvers would leave the aircraft in a very slow, low-energy, flying condition. Had an aircraft not gotten a successful hit on its target in the course of its first maneuver, that same maneuver might leave it more vulnerable to counter-attack from its opponent. In addition, thrust-vectoring had proven most effective in high-power, low-speed conditions. If an aircraft were built to be dependent on thrust-vectoring, how stable and controllable would it be if the pilot retarded the throttles?[3]

Yet the decision not to include multi-axis thrust-vectoring on the JSF does not mean the end of this technological path, or that the technology will never be incorporated into future fighters, or even retrofitted into existing designs. For one thing, the effectiveness of the new short-range missiles and helmet-mounted displays has yet to be proven in combat.[4] And while the JSF, Eurofighter, and updated Gripen fighters all lack multi-axis thrust-vectoring capability, the Russians are now offering a three-dimensional thrust-vectoring nozzle on the Sukhoi Su-30. Not all of the Sukhoi customers are requesting the capability, but the Indian Air Force already has decided to include multi-axis thrust-vectoring engines in Su-30 fighters it acquires.[5] If the concept of thrust-vectoring continues to gain international appeal in fighter aircraft designs, the U.S. and other European nations may opt to integrate the technology in their armed forces, as well.

Other factors may eventually encourage implementation of multi-axis thrust-vectoring in aircraft designs. In 2000, the U.S. Navy, the German procurement agency BWB, Boeing, and EADS (formerly MBB) funded a $60 million follow-on flight research program with the X-31 to investigate use of three-dimensional thrust-vectoring to create Extreme Short Take Off and Landing (ESTOL) capability in fighter aircraft. The hope is that use of thrust-vectoring might allow a Navy fighter to approach a carrier at a much steeper angle of attack and slower airspeed, reducing the amount of energy involved in carrier landings. Researchers continue looking at the potential of thrust-vectoring to increase fuel efficiency or reduce the fatigue life, radar observability, or even the infrared signature of fighter aircraft. Controllability

---

[3] This is clearly an important issue that would need to be resolved in order to develop an aircraft dependent on thrust-vectoring for stability and control. But it isn't necessarily insurmountable. The X-44A studies, for example, looked at possibly reprogramming the throttle control from simply increasing or decreasing thrust to a request for longitudinal acceleration or deceleration. Pulling back on the throttle would send a signal to the system that the pilot wished to decelerate the vehicle. The system could then use other methods, such as speed brakes, to slow down the vehicle while keeping the thrust level at an acceptable level to maintain stability and control.

[4] While unproven in combat, a helmet-mounted sighting system produced in the USSR seemed effective. Flying against a MiG-29 on the air combat maneuvering range, American pilots simulated close-in combat against the Russian short-range air-to-air missile

(AAM). To their surprise and dismay, when they were targeted by the Russian helmet mounted sight the American pilots lost every single such encounter.

[5] Young, interviewed by author, 25 October 2001; Stuart Penny, defense editor, *Flight International*, interviewed by author, 17 December 2001; Stuart Penney, "Different Approach," *Flight International*, Vol., 160, No. 4803, 23-29 October 2001; Bessette, interviewed by author, 10 August 2001; Tom Lawrence, Senior Aerodynamics Specialist, NavAir, Patuxent River Naval Air Station (MD), interviewed by author, 21 September 2001.

[6] Young, interviewed by author, 25 October 2001; Lawrence, interviewed by author, 21 September 2001; "X-Planes," *Flight International*, 23-29 October 2001, 38-39.

and stall-spin prevention also could continue to be a factor in future thrust-vectoring usage.[6]

The process of aircraft technology research, development, and application is rarely a simple or linear one. Even if a technology proves effective in research flight tests, it still must "buy its way onto" production aircraft designs. It must either fill what is perceived to be an important need or offer enough benefits to outweigh its costs–costs that can range from the strictly monetary to added complexity, weight, training requirements, or new problems introduced by the new technology. And in a constantly changing political and technical world, these factors too are perpetually shifting.

Incorporating a new technology into a production aircraft design also can be a matter of timing. Design phases for both the Eurofighter and the F-22 Advanced Tactical Fighter were too far along for multi-axis thrust-vectoring to be considered.[7] It may take evolution of another generation of aircraft before the technology is incorporated into a design. Or it may take development of additional new technology or a new operational requirement for which thrust-vectoring is best suited.

Thrust-vectoring's uncertain status is not a peculiar event in aeronautical research, nor is it the first time a concept investigated through NASA flight research took awhile to be applied in production aircraft. The National Advisory Committee for Aeronautics (NACA, which became NASA in 1958) and the Air Force had flight-tested variable-sweep wing technology with the X-5 in the early 1950s. But it wasn't until the outboard wing pivot was designed in the mid-1950s that the technology became practical. And even then, it wasn't until 1962, when the Air Force needed a long-range fighter/bomber that could fly supersonically yet could land on unprepared strips, that variable-sweep wing technology was incorporated into the design for the General Dynamics F-111 fighter/bomber. As Joseph Chambers, the first chairman of the High Alpha

Technology Program steering committee, said, "The real success story of NASA has been our ability to fund research so that researchers could go and evolve and mature these concepts so they were ready when the country needed them, 10 or 15 years later."[8]

But even if its specific applications remain to be seen, the thrust-vectoring research conducted with the F-18 HARV, the X-31, and the F-15 ACTIVE was unquestionably both successful and valuable. The F-18 HARV allowed engineers and researchers to explore the world of high-alpha flight–a realm that had never before been modeled or even well understood. The HATP refined existing models and provided important validation and confidence in computational codes, wind tunnel and mathematical predictions, and design tools and methods for high-alpha flight. These advancements will allow aircraft designers to better predict the high-alpha behavior of new designs, which will allow them in turn to improve both the safety and performance of future fighter aircraft. Research with the F-18 HARV, X-31, and F-15 ACTIVE also allowed engineers to investigate and develop better flight control laws, instrumentation, and systems for researching or using thrust-vectoring on future aircraft.

The three NASA thrust-vectoring projects had different objectives, but all had one thing in common: the challenges and benefits of actually taking an idea to flight. Hugh Dryden, for whom the Dryden Flight Research Center is named, once said that flight research separated "the real from the imagined."[9] Taking a concept to flight quickly separates imagined problems from those that are critical to a technology or aircraft in actual flight. X-31 researchers, for example, found to their dismay that an unheated pitot tube could become a single-point failure–a critical problem that caused the crash of one of the two X-31 research aircraft. Not all lessons in flight research are so harsh, but all three thrust-vectoring flight research programs uncovered important and unexpected problems that

[7] "The X-31: The First International US/German Experimental Program," Deutsche Aerospace publication, undated, DFRC Historical Reference Collection; Chambers, *Partners in Freedom*, 161-162. (The requirements for the Advanced Tactical Fighter were issued in 1985, while the multi-axis thrust-vectoring research projects were all in the planning and early development stages. The F-22 first flew in September 1990, 13 days before the X-31's first flight and three and a half months before the F-18 HARV's first flight with its thrust-vectoring paddles and control system.)

[8] Chambers, interviewed by author, 15 August 2001; Hallion and Gorn, *On the Frontier*, 52; Taylor, ed., *Jane's Encyclopedia of Aviation*, (New York: Portland House, 1989), 417-418.

[9] "Introductory Remarks," *Research-Airplane-Committee Report on Conference on the Progress of the X-15 Project*, NACA Compilation of Papers (Langley Aeronautical Laboratory, VA, October 25-26, 1956), xix.

needed resolution in order to make the flights and programs successful. That knowledge, in turn, will make incorporation of thrust-vectoring less risky for manufacturers wanting to utilize the technology in the future.

Taking an idea to flight also separates the real from the imagined in another, equally important way. Until the F-18 HARV and X-31 demonstrated successful thrust-vectoring techniques and capabilities in actual flight, thrust-vectoring was merely an interesting concept, an imagined solution to a desire for better maneuverability and controllability. Once the two aircraft had flown and, in particular, once the X-31 had demonstrated its stunning capability in dramatic low-altitude maneuvers at the 1995 Paris Air Show, the technology was no longer something that worked in imagination or theory. It was real. The debate changed, the view of the horizon shifted, the world of possibilities suddenly became significantly broader.

The explorations made in the F-18 HARV, X-31, and F-15 ACTIVE thrust-vectoring research projects proved that the technology was viable and provided invaluable information about the aerodynamic, propulsion, flight control, and design considerations the new technology both required and allowed. The door is now open for future engineers to explore the wider frontier of ways in which knowledge and technology can be further advanced.

These three flight research programs are illuminating on several levels. Viewed individually, each offers valuable information about both multi-axis thrust-vectoring technology and the successful management and execution of flight research projects. Collectively, they also provide insights into the complex factors surrounding not just the organization, funding, and execution of research programs, but also the application of new technology developed or tested through that research.

The F-18 HARV, the X-31, and the F-15 ACTIVE were productive research programs. Individually and collectively, they significantly expanded the field of knowledge about both thrust-vectoring and high-alpha flight and developed and helped validate design tools, methods, hardware, and software. They also successfully demonstrated a variety of potential benefits that thrust-vectoring offered in terms of safety, maneuverability, low-observability, and efficiency of fighter aircraft. And yet military interest in the technology seemed to wane throughout the 1990s; multi-axis thrust-vectoring has yet to be incorporated into any operational U.S. or German aircraft. While the Lockheed-Martin Joint Strike Fighter–the newest U.S. military fighter to gain development approval– has the capacity to vector its thrust to some extent, its system is designed primarily for vertical-landing capability rather than for increased maneuverability or high-alpha performance. And although some of the lessons Pratt & Whitney engineers learned through the ACTIVE program helped them resolve similar issues with the three-bearing swivel nozzle design for the JSF engine, the thrust-vectoring system eventually incorporated into the JSF did not really evolve from, or bear much resemblance to, the various multi-axis thrust-vectoring systems researched by NASA and its partners.[10]

If research results exhibited significant benefits inherent in the technology, why hasn't it been applied? There are several reasons, but the biggest is simply that aeronautical research doesn't occur in a vacuum. External world and national events, priorities, and politics influence the birth and cancellation of research programs and the eventual application of new technology as much as the inherent worth of any concept or technology itself. The development of new engine technology and shifting military priorities and concerns helped launch the various thrust-vectoring research efforts in the 1980s. But changes in military concerns and priorities during the 1990s, as well as development of new missile technology, converged to work against a concept that had been heralded with great enthusiasm only a decade before.

After placing such emphasis on improved maneuverability and high-alpha performance in fighter planes, why weren't U.S. military officials more eager to see multi-axis thrust-vectoring technology applied? After all, the technology had been proven through four flight research programs and all indications were that thrust-vectoring would solve the problems that seemed so pressing in the decade following the Vietnam War. So why it was it not put into practical application?

[10] Bruce Wood, Pratt & Whitney, interviewed by the author, 24 April 2002.

There are several reasons.

The first, and perhaps foremost, has to do with the F-22 Raptor and design cycles. The F-22 design was finalized before engine manufacturers developed axisymmetric, multi-axis thrust-vectoring nozzles and before the X-31, the HARV, or the F-16 MATV took flight. The Raptor's design incorporated two-dimensional thrust-vectoring, which was state-of-the-art in engine control at the time and had been flight tested in the Air Force F-15 S/MTD program. But once the Air Force had committed to the F-22, protecting funding and support for that program–especially in a time of decreasing military budgets–became a high priority. The F-22 was a supersonic, stealthy, Cold War fighter designed to fire missiles beyond visual range (BVR). It was maneuverable, but not as maneuverable as a fighter with multi-axis thrust-vectoring capability would be. The prevailing philosophy in the Air Force had become, once again, that speed, stealth, and the capability to fire missiles beyond visual range amounted to a fighter's best defense.

There were still those within both military and industry who argued that while the BVR strategy worked in theory, the rules of engagement for any conflict could very well require visual identification of a target, as they did both in Vietnam and in the Gulf War. To abide by those rules, a fighter would end up fighting close-in combat, where high-alpha performance and extreme maneuverability could once again become critical factors. Even in such a scenario, some in the military argued, use of thrust-vectoring for post-stall maneuvering would leave a fighter in an extremely slow and vulnerable position, especially in a multiple-bogey fight.

Others–particularly pilots who had flown the X-31 or MATV–countered that pilots had only to learn how and when to employ thrust-vectoring in order to maintain the upper hand in a conflict. There is a case to be made on either side of the argument. But an undeniable factor in all those arguments was the fact that the high-tech F-22 was the crown jewel of the Air Force's future force strategy, and wasn't designed for a slow, close-in, post-stall dogfight. If the Air Force supported extreme maneuverability as an important priority, the F-22 might begin to seem a less-than-ideal choice, and the F-22 was already

encountering enough resistance. With a price tag approaching $100 million per copy, the "affordable" F-22 was becoming vulnerable to attack from critics who thought there must be a more cost-effective way of attaining improved fighter performance.

Into this embattled procurement environment came the advocates of multi-axis thrust-vectoring. They argued not only that there were benefits to incorporating multi-axis thrust-vectoring into new aircraft designs, but also that many of the technology's benefits could be realized by retrofitting existing front-line fighters with thrust-vectoring capability. But if the performance of an F-15 or F-16 could be significantly improved simply by adding a thrust-vectoring engine nozzle, it might be argued that the expensive F-22 was unneeded. There were, of course, other high-tech aspects of the F-22 that couldn't be replicated with a modified F-15, such as its stealth capability. Still, because of the timing of its development, multi-axis thrust-vectoring became a threat to the F-22 instead of being simply a new and promising performance-enhancing technology.

Another reason for the military's lukewarm embrace of thrust-vectoring for existing or new fighters was the development of better missile and targeting technology. Among driving forces behind multi-axis thrust-vectoring and post-stall maneuvering was a desire to take advantage of short-range missiles that could lock onto an adversary's frontal aspect. But by the late 1990s, the development of helmet-mounted displays and more maneuverable "off-boresight" missiles offered another solution to attacking adversaries not directly in a fighter's line of sight. Using a helmet-mounted targeting display, a fighter pilot could lock onto a target that was off to one side and fire an "off-boresight" missile, such as the AIM-9X, which would then turn to and track the selected target. Rather than going to the expense and complexity of making an entire aircraft more maneuverable, the new displays and missiles offered the military the option of simply making its missiles more maneuverable.

"Off-boresight" missiles and helmet-mounted displays are new concepts, still unproven in combat. Proponents of thrust-vectoring technology argue that the effectiveness of the missiles decreases as they maneuver to a target, so the optimal combination would still be to make *both* the aircraft and the missiles more maneuverable.[11] But incorporating more maneuverable missiles could offer a less complex and expensive approach to the problem of close-in combat maneuverability.[12]

Beyond Maneuverability

Researchers were aware of the winds of change stirring in both the air-combat philosophy and the procurement offices of the U.S. Air Force even as various multi-axis thrust-vectoring research programs were being conducted and engine manufacturers were proceeding with the development of axisymmetric thrust-vectoring nozzles. In the 10 years between 1982, when the X-31 program was first outlined, and 1992, when the ACTIVE program was first proposed, high-alpha maneuvering ceased to be a driving concern within the U.S. military. So ACTIVE program researchers made a point of focusing on other areas, such as efficiency, in an effort to demonstrate other benefits to thrust-vectoring technology beyond high-alpha maneuverability. And while the ACTIVE testbed was able to demonstrate a 4 percent improvement in fuel efficiency and range through use of thrust-vectoring in cruise flight, that alone wasn't going to be enough for the technology to be adopted in either an existing or new aircraft design.

It gradually became clear to researchers that multi-axis thrust-vectoring's real value, at least in terms of winning support for its application in military aircraft, might lie in the possibilities it offered for radically new aircraft designs. The ability to integrate multi-axis thrust-vectoring into an aircraft's flight control system opened up the possibility of using an aircraft's propulsion system to perform some of the stability and control functions of other aircraft components. With yaw control provided by a thrust-vectoring engine, an aircraft's vertical tail could be reduced in size or

possibly eliminated altogether. Even control surfaces could be eliminated if the aircraft's propulsion system could assume their function.

Such radical design ideas offered several advantages. Reducing an aircraft's vertical tail reduced its radar cross-section, thereby improving its stealth characteristics. Reducing the size of components or eliminating moving parts would also reduce the weight and complexity of an aircraft, further improving its performance. Researchers recognized these potential benefits, which is what led to the numerous tailless flight research projects conducted or proposed between 1995 and 2000. But to date, no funding has materialized for any of these tailless research projects.

There are legitimate concerns about designing an aircraft that would be dependent on its propulsion system for basic stability and control. High on this list of concerns is the complete reliance on computer control of the aircraft systems, including the engine. Computer-dependent aircraft, of course, have been in existence for more than 20 years. The F-16, the F-18, and even the radical forward-swept wing X-29 all were based on inherently unstable designs, meaning that if their computerized flight control systems failed, the aircraft would spin out of control. To prevent such an occurrence, designers simply incorporated redundant computers into the aircraft's flight control systems; if an aircraft has three or four computers on board, the chances that all of them will fail are remote.

The solution becomes far more complicated, however, if it is not simply a computer but the aircraft's engine itself that is critical for basic stability and control. In any single-engine fighter, such as the F-16 or even the new JSF, a working engine is essential for flight. Yet even if an F-16 pilot has an engine flameout he will generally have enough basic control of the aircraft to either attempt a relight of the engine or a safe ejection. But if the engine is providing basic stability and control for the aircraft, in addition to

---

[11] Russian aircraft manufacturers and their customers do not necessarily feel this way. During the AERO India Airshow in 2003, five Sukhoi Su-30MK1s took part in the opening day flypast. The Su-30MK1 has two thrust-vectoring engines with nozzles that swivel 360 degrees, along with the latest helmet mounted sight. India announced plans to manufacture 130 of this aircraft type, with the engines coming from Russia. *AviationWeek* March 2003, 77.

[12] Tom Lawrence, NavAir, interviewed by the author, 21 Sep-

tember 2001; Young, X-31 interviewed by the author, 25 October 2001; Francis, interviewed by the author, 14 February 2002; Doane, interviewed by the author, 29 April 2002; Mike Gerzanics, interviewed by the author, 2 April 2002; Schkolnik, interviewed by the author, 30 March 2001; Penny, interviewed by the author, 17 December 2001; Smith, interviewed by the author, 16 February 2002; Knox, interviewed by the author, 1 October 2001; Ross, interviewed by the author, 18 February 2002; Wood, interviewed by the author, 24 April 2002; James Fallows, "Uncle Sam Buys an Airplane," *The Atlantic Monthly*, June 2002, 62-74.

thrust, a flameout becomes a much more serious issue, one that might not leave a pilot with enough time to eject safely. And unlike what may be done with flight control computers, it is impractical to incorporate three or four engines into an aircraft design to protect against a potential problem with one.

Another challenge to be overcome with a design dependent on thrust-vectoring involves what happens if and when a pilot reduces power. At idle thrust, insufficient force is available to provide aircraft stability or control. This is a concern even in using thrust-vectoring to assist steep, slow landing approaches, but it would become an even greater issue in a design dependent on the propulsion system for basic stability and control.

Does all this mean that incorporating thrust-vectoring as a flight-critical element of an aircraft's design will never become a reality? Not necessarily. But it does suggest that there are issues to resolve before such a design shift will happen. The prospect presents designers with the challenge of building an aircraft engine as reliable as the wing attach points, or designing some type of backup system that will provide enough control to allow for either an engine relight or a safe ejection. The risks of a propulsion-dependent design also mean that the first application of the concept may be in Uninhabited Aerial Vehicles (UAVs) such as the X-45A, as opposed to in piloted aircraft.[13]

[13] Gerzanics, interviewed by the author, 2 April 2002; Doane, interviewed by the author, 29 April 2002; Schkolnik, interviewed by the author, 30 March 2001; Ross, interviewed by the author, 18 February 2002; Guy Norris, interviewed by the author, 11 January 2002; Wood, interviewed by the author, 24 April 2002; Bursey, interviewed by the author, 26 April 2002; Knox, interviewed by the author, 1 October 2001.

Bibliography

Sources

Unless otherwise indicated, primary materials, including tape recordings of interviews, are on file in the Dryden Flight Research Center Historical Reference Collection, Edwards, California

Interviews

Bessette, Denis. Interviewed by Lane E. Wallace, 10 August 2001.

Bundick, Tom. Interviewed by Lane E. Wallace, 14 August 2001.

Burcham, Frank W. Interviewed by the Lane E. Wallace, 24 August 1995.

Bursey, Roger. Interviewed by the Lane E. Wallace, 26 April 2002.

Chambers, Joseph R. Interviewed by Lane E. Wallace, 15 August 2001.

Flick, Brad. Interviewed by Lane E. Wallace, 22 August 2001.

Foster, John. Interviewed by Lane E. Wallace, 14 August 2001.

Francis, Col. Michael, USAF (Ret.). Interviewed by Lane E. Wallace, 14 February 2002.

Gatlin, Donald. Interviewed by Lane E. Wallace, 14 August 2001.

Gera, Joe. Interviewed by Lane E. Wallace, 8 August 2001.

Gerzanics, Mike. Interviewed by the Lane E. Wallace, 2 April 2002.

Gilbert, William P. nterviewed by Lane E. Wallace, 13 August 2001.

Huber, Peter. Interviewed by the Lane E. Wallace, 7 February 2002.

Knox, Fred. Interviewed by the Lane E. Wallace, 1 October 2001.

Law, Peter. Interviewed by Lane E. Wallace, 17 December 2001.

Lawrence, Tom. Interviewed by Lane E. Wallace, 21 September 2001.

Meyer, Robert. Interviewed by Lane E. Wallace, 9 August 2001.

Murri, Dan. Interviewed by Lane E. Wallace, 14 August 2001.

Pahle, Joe. Interviewed by Lane E. Wallace, 16 August 2001.

Penny, Stuart. Interviewed by Lane E. Wallace, 17 December 2001.

Perry, John. Interviewed by the Lane E. Wallace, 6 February 2002.

Ray, Ron. Interviewed by Lane E. Wallace, 17 August 2001.

Robinson, Michael. Interviewed by the Lane E. Wallace, 15 February 2002 and 27 March 2002.

Ross, Hannes. Interviewed by the Lane E. Wallace, 18 February 2002.

Schellenger, Harvey. Interviewed by the Lane E. Wallace, 5 February 2002.

Schkolnik, Gerard. Interviewed by Lane E. Wallace, 30 March 2001.

Schkolnik, Gerard and James Smolka. Interviewed by the Lane E. Wallace, 8 May 2001.

Schneider, Ed. Interviewed by Lane E. Wallace, 10, 24 August 2001.

Sheen, John. Interviewed by the Lane E. Wallace, 11 March 2002.

Smith, Rogers. Interviewed by the Lane E. Wallace, 16 February 2002.

Szalai, Kenneth J. Interviewed by the Lane E. Wallace, 6 March 2002.

Trippensee, Gary. Interviewed by the Lane E. Wallace, 13 August 2002.

Wood, Bruce. Interviewed by the Lane E. Wallace, 24 April 2002.

Young, Jennifer. Interviewed by Lane E. Wallace, 25 October 2001.

Books and Articles

AviationWeek. (March 2003): 77.

Brown, Alan. "F-15 Thrusts to Almost Mach 2." *The X-Press* 6 (December 1996).

Chambers, Joseph R. *Partners in Freedom*. Washington, D.C.: NASA Monographs in Aerospace History, 2000.

Cook, Nick. "NASA Looks To New X-44A For Tailless Experimental Research." *Janes Defense Weekly* (6 October 1999): 5.

Dornheim, Michael A. "Paris Flight to Cap Busy X-31

Test Schedule." *Aviation Week & Space Technology* (12 June 1995).

Fallows, James. "Uncle Sam Buys an Airplane." *The Atlantic Monthly* (June 2002): 62-74.

Hallion, Richard P. and Michael H. Gorn *On the Frontier: Experimental Flight at NASA Dryden.* 2nd ed. Washington, D.C.: Smithsonian Books, 2003.

Henderson, Breck W. "Dryden Completes First Flights of F-18 HARV with Thrust Vectoring." *Aviation Week & Space Technology* (29 July 199): 25.

Hunley, J.D. "NASA Tests New Nozzle to Improve Performance." *The X-Press* Vol. 38: 4, (April 1996): 1.

Kearns, Sean. "Experimental Aircraft May Be On Horizon." *Antelope Valley Press* (11 July 1999): A-1, A-8.

Lewis, Paul. "Lockheed-Martin: The Fort Worth Fighter." *Flight International* supplement (5-11 September 2000): 25-30.

Lopez, Ramon. "ACTIVE Takes Step To Propulsion Control." *Flight International* (23 December 1998 – 5 January 1999).

Mark, Hans and Arnold Levine. *The Management of Research Institutions: A Look at Government Laboratories.* Washington, D.C.: National Aeronautics and Space Administration, SP-481, 1984.

Norris, Guy. "NASA will use its HARV F-18 to tackle 'falling leaf' problem." *Flight International* (19-25 June 1996): 22.

_____. "Thunder in the Desert." *Flight International* (supplement), (5-11 September 2000), 32-35.

Penney, Stuart. "Different Approach." *Flight International* Vol., 160, No. 4803, (23-29 October 2001).

Phillips, Edward H. "NASA Langley Drop Model Explores X-31A High-Alpha, Post-Stall Flight." *Aviation Week & Space Technology* (2 March 1992).

Smith, Bruce A. "F-15 ACTIVE Tests Supersonic Yaw Vectoring." *Aviation Week & Space Technology* (29 April, 1996).

Taylor, Michael J.H. ed. *Jane's Encyclopedia of Aviation.* New York: Portland House, 1989.

Tomayko, James E. *Computers Take Flight: A History of NASA's Pioneering Digital Fly-by-Wire Project.* Washington, D.C.: National Aeronautics and Space Administration, NASA SP-4224, 2000.

"X-Planes." *Flight International* (23-29 October 2001): 38-39.

"X-31 Experimental Aircraft Flies Again at Pax River." *Aerospace Daily* (28 February 2001).

"1996 Design & Engineering Awards." *Popular Mechanics* (January 1996).

Reports and Technical Papers

ACTIVE AdAPT Sensor Study Objectives and Requirements. 7 December 1993. DFRC Historical Reference Collection.

Advanced Control Technology For Integrated Vehicles (ACTIVE) Phase 2B Flight Test Plan. NASA Dryden Flight Research Center document, 24 June 1997.

Bosworth, John T. and C. Stoliker. "The X-31A Quasi-Tailless Flight Test Results." NASA TP-3624, June 1996.

Bowers, Albion H. et. al. "An Overview of the NASA F-18 High Alpha Research Vehicle." NASA TM-4772, Edwards, CA, 1996.

_____. "F-18 High Alpha Research Vehicle: A 1995 Overview." Draft, from Al Bowers personal files.

Burcham, Frank W. Jr., et. al. "Propulsion Flight Research at NASA Dryden from 1967 to 1997." NASA TP-206554, July 1998.

Bursey, Roger. "The F-15 ACTIVE Aircraft, The Next Step." Final draft of AIAA paper, 1995. DFRC Historical Reference Collection.

Cobleigh, Brent R. "High-Angle-of-Attack Yawing Moment Asymmetry of the X-31 Aircraft from Flight Test." NASA CR- 186030, September 1994.

Conners, Timothy R. and Robert L. Sims. "Full Flight Envelope Direct Thrust Measurement on a Supersonic Aircraft." NASA TM-1998-206560, July 1998.

Del Frate, John H. and Fanny A. Zuniga. "In-flight Flow Field Analysis on the NASA F-18 High Alpha Research Vehicle with Comparisons to Ground Facility Data." Paper, AIAA-90-0231, presented at the American Institute of Aeronautics and Astronautics 28th Aerospace Sciences Meeting, Reno, NV, 8–11 January 1990.

Doane, P. et. al, "F-15 ACTIVE: A Flexible Propulsion Integration Testbed." Paper presented at the 30th

AIAA/ASME/SAE/ASEE Joint Propulsion Conference, Indianapolis, IN, June 27-29, 1994.

Erickson, Gary E. "Wind Tunnel Investigation of Vortex Flows on F-18 Configuration at Subsonic Through Transonic Speeds." NASA TP-3111, December 1991.

Eubanks, D. et. al. "X-31 CIC Flight Test Results." Viewgraphs, from Full Envelope Agility Workshop Briefing, Eglin AFB, FL, March 1995. DFRC Historical Reference Collection.

"Extreme Attitude and Rate Inlet Flow Research." Draft HATP document, 10 July 1987. DFRC Historical Reference Collection.

Fisher, David F., et. al. "Effect of Actuated Forebody Strakes on the Forebody Aerodynamics of the NASA F-18 HARV." NASA TM-4774, October 1996.

Fisher, David F. et. al. "Summary of In-flight Flow Visualization Obtained From the NASA High Alpha Research Vehicle." NASA TM-101734, January 1991.

Final Report for Period October 1984 to 31 August 1991. STOL/Maneuver Technology Demonstrator, Volume 1, Executive Summary, WL-TR-91-3080, 30 September 1991.

Flight Research Objectives of NASA in the X-31 Enhanced Fighter Maneuverability (EFM) Program, (n.d.). DFRC Historical Reference Collection.

"Flight Test Plan: HARV NASA-1 Control Law Evaluation," draft, 1 October 1992. DFRC Historical Reference Collection.

"F-14/F-110 High Angle of Attack Flight Tests." SETP 32nd Symposium Proceedings, ISSN# 0742-3705, Los Angeles, CA, October 1988.

"F-15 Advanced Control Technology for Integrated Vehicles (ACTIVE) Project Plan," 12 April 1994. DFRC Historical Reference Collection.

"F-18 HARV Objectives and Requirements Document T: "High Alpha Thrust Degradation and Prediction Study," 27 August 1993 update. DFRC Historical Reference Collection.

"F-18 HARV Objectives and Requirements Document XX: Propulsion Inlet Research," 20 April 1993. DFRC Historical Reference Collection.

"F-18 HARV Propulsion Research." ARTS Review viewgraphs, 7 January 1993.

"F-18 HARV Real-Time Thrust Method (RTTM),"

viewgraphs, from XRP 1994 Annual Report, Ron Ray, P.I. DFRC Historical Reference Collection.

"F-18 High Angle of Attack Flight Test Plan." Ames Research Center and Dryden Flight Research Facility Document HA 86-301, November 1986.

"F-18 High Angle-of-Attack Flight Test Plan." HA 86-301, Ames Research Center, Dryden Flight Research Facility, November 1986.

"F-18 High Angle-of-Attack Flight Test Plan." HA 86-301 Revision A, Ames Research Center, Dryden Flight Research Facility, August 1987.

"F-18 High Alpha Research Vehicle Program Objectives and Requirements Document HH," 1 October 1992.

"F-18 Objectives and Requirements Specification Document F: Flight Control and Flying Qualities Study," 5 May 1987. DFRC Historical Reference Collection.

F-18 Objective and Requirements Specification, 29 May 1987, and "Document H," 5 August 1987. DFRC Historical Reference Collection.

F-18 #840 HARV Flight Chronology. DFRC Historical Reference Collection.

Groves, Al, Cmdr. et. al. "X-31 Flight Test Update." Society of Experimental Test Pilots Thirty-seventh Symposium Proceedings, ISSN #0742-3705, Los Angeles, CA, September 1993.

HARV Tech Brief II-7. 14 July 1992.

HARV Research Equipment. Viewgraph, (n.d.). DFRC Historical Reference Collection.

High Alpha Technology Program (HATP) Plan. 19 March 1990.

High Alpha Research Vehicle Phase II Flight Test Plan. HA90-70-202, June 1990. DFRC Historical Reference Collection.

Hreha, M. et. al. "An Approach to Aircraft Performance Optimization Using Thrust-vectoring." AIAA paper 94-3361. Presented at the 30th AIAA/ASMESAE/ASEE Joint Propulsion Conference, Indianapolis, IN, 27-29 June 1994.

"Introductory Remarks." *Research-Airplane-Committee Report on Conference on the Progress of the X-15 Project* NACA Compilation of Papers. Langley Aeronautical Laboratory, VA, October 25-26, 1956.

"JAST Technology Maturation Utilizing the X-31 Testbed," briefing papers, VMS-BRF-95-06.

Knox, Fred D. and Thomas C. Santangelo. "Taking an X-Airplane to the Paris Air Show." Presentation to The Society of Experimental Test Pilots. Beverly Hills, CA, 29 September 1995.

Lackey, J. and Lt. D. Prater, USN. "Limited Navy Flying Qualities and Performance Evaluation of the NASA F-18 HARV." NASA TM-93-11 SA, 21 June 1993.

Murri, Daniel G. et. al, "Flight-Test Results of Actuated Forebody Strake Controls on the F-18 High alpha Research Vehicle." Presented at the High-Angle-of-Attack Technology Conference. NASA Langley Research Center, Hampton, VA, 17-19 September 1996.

"NASA X-31 Mishap Investigation Report." 18 August 1995.

"NASA X-31 Mishap Investigation." Viewgraphs, from briefing by Guy Gardner, Board Chairperson, to Ken Szalai, Director, Dryden Flight Research Center, 2 March 1995.

"NASA High Alpha Technology Program: Overview/Status/Plans/Deliverables." Viewgraphs of presentation for HATP Industry/DOD Tour, May-June 1993. DFRC Historical Reference Collection.

Navy/NASA Loan Agreement For F-18 Aircraft. 21 May 1986. DFRC Historical Reference Collection.

Nguyen, Luat T. "Summary of 1993 HATP Industry/DOD Tour." Viewgraphs, 8 July 1993. DFRC Historical Reference Collection.

Orme, John S. et. al. "Development and Testing of a High Stability Engine Control (HISTEC) System." NASA TM-206562, July 1998.

Orme John S. and Robert L. Sims. "Selected Performance Measurements of the F-15 ACTIVE Axisymmetric Thrust-Vectoring Nozzle." Paper, presented at the 14th ISABE (International Society for Air Breathing Engines) Annual Symposium, IS 166. Florence, Italy, 5-10 September 1999.

"Project Test Plan #1573." Naval Air Warfare Center Aircraft Division Flight Test and Engineering Group, unclassified document, 7 March 1994. DFRC Historical Reference Collection.

Propulsion and Performance Branch 1993-1994 Biennial Report. DFRC Historical Reference Collection.

Radio Transcript from X-31 Accident. DFRC Historical Reference Collection.

Regenie, Victoria, et. al, "The F-18 High Alpha Research Vehicle: A High-Angle-of-Attack Testbed Aircraft." AIAA paper AIAA-92-4121, presented at the 6th AIAA Biennial Flight Test Conference. Hilton Head Island, SC, 24-26 August 1992.

Richwine, David. and David. Fisher. "In-flight Leading-Edge Extension Vortex Flow-Field Survey Measurements on a F-18 Aircraft at High Angle of Attack." AIAA paper AIAA-91-3248, presented at the AIAA 9th Applied Aerodynamics Conference, Baltimore, MD, 23-25 September 1991.

Rollout. MBB Publication. 1 March 1990. DFRC Historical Reference Collection.

Schkolnik, Gerard S. "Integrated Control Systems for Aircraft and Turbine Engines, Research Status, Performance Seeking Controls, Flight Test Programs." Presentation viewgraphs, UTSI Aero-Propulsion Systems Technology, Test and Evaluation Short Course, 16 April 1997. DFRC Historical Reference Collection.

Schkolnik, Gerard and Jim Smolka, "F-15 Advanced Control Technology for Integrated Vehicles." Paper presented at the Royal Aeronautical Society's 1999 Fighter Conference, England, 30 September 1999. Gerard Schkolnik personal files.

Smolka, James, et. al, "ACTIVE F-15 Flight Research Program." SETP 40th Annual Symposium Proceedings. ISSN#0742-3705, Beverly Hills, CA, September 1996.

Southwick, Robert D. High Stability Engine Control (HISTEC): Phase IIIB Final Report. NASA CR-209315, August 1999.

Stoliker, Patrick C. and John T. Bosworth. "Evaluation of High-Angle-of-Attack Handling Qualities for the X-31A Using Standard Evaluation Maneuvers." NASA TM-104322, September 1996.

Stoliker, P.C. "High-Angle-of-Attack Handling Qualities Predictions and Criteria Evaluation for the X-31A." NASA TM-4758, March 1997.

Sweeney, Joseph E. and Major Michael A. Gerzanics. "F-16 Multi-Axis Thrust Vectoring Program." SETP Thirty-seventh Symposium Proceedings, ISSN# 0742-3705, Beverly Hills, CA, September 1993.

_____. "F-16 MATV Envelope Expansion." Presentation to the Thirty-eighth Symposium of The Society of Experimental Test Pilots, Beverly Hills,

CA, September 1994.

Tamrat, B.F. et. al, "X-31 Quasi-Tailless Flight Test Experiment. Final Report." TFD-95-1261, draft, 9 June 1995. DFRC Historical Reference Collection.

Tavella, Domingo A., et. al, "Pneumatic Vortical Flow Control at High Angles of Attack." AIAA Paper 90-0098, presented at the 28th Aerospace Sciences Meeting, Reno, NV, 8–11 January 1990.

"The X-31: The First International US/German Experimental Program." Deutsche Aerospace Publication, (n.d.). DFRC Historical Reference Collection.

Walker, Larry et. al, "ACTIVE F-15 Flight Research Program. Paper presented at the SETP 40th Annual Symposium. Beverly Hills, CA, September 1996.

Williams, David. et. al, "Comparison of Flight and Sub-scale Model Wing Rock Characteristics of an F-18 Aircraft." Final Report for NASA Grant NCA2-513, University of Notre Dame, 30 April 1993.

"X-31A: 'Barrier Breaker for the 21st Century," Rockwell document, DFRC Historical Reference Collection.

"X-31 Enhanced Fighter Maneuverability Program Final Report, Volume 1." Videotape recording, from Michael Francis personal files.

X-31 Flight Report 1-214. 10 March 1994; 1-215, 10 March 1994; 1-216, 10 March 1994.

X-31/JAST FMIPT Meeting, 16 November 1994. Viewgraphs. DFRC Historical Reference Collection.

X-31 Post-Stall Envelope Expansion and Tactical Utility Testing. Presentation by Dave Canter, NAWC-AD, at the Fourth High Alpha Conference, NASA Dryden Flight Research Center, 13-14 July 1994. NASA Conference Publication 10143, Volume 2.

X-31 Program Close-Out Briefing. Viewgraph presentation to Dr. Robert Whitehead, Associate Administrator of Aeronautics, NASA, 3 November 1995.

X-31 Total Estimated Development Costs, 24 March 1995. DFRC Historical Reference Collection.

Unpublished Sources

Ayers, Ted to Col. John "Tack" Nix, correspondence regarding Ames-Dryden interest in supporting the X-31 program, undated draft, DFRC Historical Reference Collection.

Chambers, Joseph R. "Questions." Email to Lane Wallace, 9 March 2002, Lane Wallace personal files. Fisher, Dave. "F-18 – What We Learned." Email to Lane Wallace, 27 August 2001, with comments by Dan Banks, Bob Hall, Jim Luckring and Dan Murri. DFRC Historical Reference Collection.

Crother, C.A. to H. Schellenger. "Yaw Control Prior to 2-73 Departure." 11 December 1992. Internal Rockwell International Letter. DFRC Historical Reference Collection.

Fisher, Dave, Dan Banks, Robert Hall, Joseph Chambers, Jim Luckring and Dan Murri. Email to Lane Wallace regarding results and lessons of the F-18 HARV program, 18 September 2001.

Buchacker, E., X-31A Flight Test Coordinator for WTD-61 to Kenneth J. Szalai, 31 January 1991 regarding WTD-61's wish to have NASA involved in the X-31 flight test program, DFRC Historical Reference Collection.

Memo. "X-31 Simulation/ITF Requirements." From Dale Mackall to Dwain Deets, et. al, 30 August 1991. DFRC Historical Reference Collection.

Memo. Donald H. Gatlin to OP/Chief, Dryden Aeronautical Projects Office, 29 April 1987. DFRC Historical Reference Collection.

Memo. Robert W. Kempel to the Society of Flight Test Engineers, Inc., nominating the F-18 HARV project/team for the 1993 "Kelly" Johnson Achievement Award, 8 March 1993.

Memo. Victoria Regenie to HARV Project leads regarding notes from participants of the industry tour, (n.d.). DFRC Historical Reference Collection.

Murri, Dan. Email to Lane Wallace regarding strake fabrication, 19 September 2001.

Ross, Hannes. "X-31 Questions." Email to Lane Wallace, 17 February 2002.

See, Guy M. to Joe Gera, correspondence regarding Tack Nix visit to discuss NASA participation in the X-31 program, 6 December 1990. DFRC Historical Reference Collection.

Steenken William G., Engine Operability and GEAE HARV Program manager, GE Aircraft Engines, to Richard Burley, NASA Lewis Research Center regarding HARV Flight Inlet Data Program, 11

January 1993. DFRC Historical Reference Collection.

_____. Engine Operability and GEAE HARV Program manager, GE Aircraft Engines, to Denis Bessette regarding significance of HARV propulsion research to, 6 January 1994, DFRC Historical Reference Collection.

Sutton, George. Email to Lane E. Wallace regarding early use of thrust-vectoring control in rocket design, 22 January 2002.

"X-31: From Roll-out to Tactical Evaluation," Deutsche Aerospace document, April 1994, from Peter Huber personal files.

"1995 X-31 Paris Air Show Trip Report." Memo, from John T. Bosworth to acting chief, Research Engineering Division, Dryden Flight Research Center, 18 July 1995, DFRC Historical Reference Collection.

Index

Documentary Histories

Exploring the Unknown

Logsdon, John M., ed., with Linda J. Lear, Jannelle Warren Findley, Ray A. Williamson, and Dwayne A. Day. *Exploring the Unknown: Selected Documents in the History of the U.S. Civil Space Program, Volume I, Organizing for Exploration*. NASA SP-4407, 1995.

Logsdon, John M., ed, with Dwayne A. Day, and Roger D. Launius. *Exploring the Unknown: Selected Documents in the History of the U.S. Civil Space Program, Volume II, External Relationships*. NASA SP-4407, 1996.

Logsdon, John M., ed., with Roger D. Launius, David H. Onkst, and Stephen J. Garber. *Exploring the Unknown: Selected Documents in the History of the U.S. Civil Space Program, Volume III, Using Space*. NASA SP-4407, 1998.

Logsdon, John M., ed., with Ray A. Williamson, Roger D. Launius, Russell J. Acker, Stephen J. Garber, and Jonathan L. Friedman. *Exploring the Unknown: Selected Documents in the History of the U.S. Civil Space Program, Volume IV, Accessing Space*. NASA SP-4407, 1999.

Logsdon, John M., ed., with Amy Paige Snyder, Roger D. Launius, Stephen J. Garber, and Regan Anne Newport. *Exploring the Unknown: Selected Documents in the History of the U.S. Civil Space Program, Volume V, Exploring the Cosmos*. NASA SP-4407, 2001.

Logsdon, John M., ed., with Stephen J. Garber, Roger D. Launius, and Ray A. Williamson. *Exploring the Unknown: Selected Documents in the History of the U.S. Civil Space Program, Volume VI: Space and Earth Science*. NASA SP-2004-4407, 2004.

The Wind and Beyond

Hansen, James R., ed. *The Wind and Beyond: Journey into the History of Aerodynamics in America, Volume 1, The Ascent of the Airplane*. NASA SP-2003-4409, 2003.

Hansen, James R., ed. *The Wind and Beyond: Journey into the History of Aerodynamics in America, Volume 2, Reinventing the Airplane*. NASA SP-2007-4409, 2007.

Brief Histories of NASA

Anderson, Frank W., Jr. *Orders of Magnitude: A History of NACA and NASA, 1915-1980*. NASA SP-4403, 1981.

Bilstein, Roger E. *Orders of Magnitude: A History of the NACA and NASA, 1915-1990*. NASA SP-4406, 1989.

Bilstein, Roger E. *Testing Aircraft, Exploring Space: An Illustrated History of NACA and NASA*. Baltimore: Johns Hopkins University Press, 2003.

Critical Issues in the History of Spaceflight

Dick, Steven J. and Launius, Roger D. *Critical Issues in the History of Spaceflight*. (NASA SP-2006-4702).

Societal Impact of Spaceflight

Dick, Steven J. and Launius, Roger D. *Societal Impact of Spaceflight.* (NASA SP-2007-4801).

Memoirs

Chertok, Boris. *Rockets and People,* Volume 1. (NASA SP-2005-4110).
 Visit http://history.nasa.gov/series95.html for a pdf versions of this document.

Chertok, Boris. *Rockets and People: Creating a Rocket Industry*, Volume II. (NASA SP-2006-4110).

Mudgway, Douglas J. William H. Pickering: America's Deep Space Pioneer. (NASA SP-2007-4113).

Aeronautics and Space Report of the President

The annual "President's Report" is a summary of the Government's aerospace activities each year. Mandated by law, it contains information on aerospace activities conducted by 14 Federal departments and agencies. It also contains an executive summary organized by agency, narrative sections organized by subject, as well as extensive appendices containing useful historical data on spacecraft launches, budget figures, key policy documents from the fiscal year, and a glossary. Visit http://history.nasa.gov/series95.html for pdf versions of these documents.

NASA Historical Data Books

Van Nimmen, Jane, and Leonard C. Bruno, with Robert L. Rosholt. *NASA Historical Data Book, Vol. I: NASA Resources, 1958-1968.* NASA SP-4012, 1976, rep. ed. 1988.

Ezell, Linda Neuman. *NASA Historical Data Book, Vol. II: Programs and Projects, 1958-1968.* NASA SP-4012, 1988.

Ezell, Linda Neuman. *NASA Historical Data Book, Vol. III: Programs and Projects, 1969-1978.* NASA SP-4012, 1988.

Gawdiak, Ihor, with Helen Fedor. *NASA Historical Data Book, Vol. IV: NASA Resources, 1969-1978.* NASA SP-4012, 1994.

Rumerman, Judy A. *NASA Historical Data Book, Vol. V: NASA Launch Systems, Space Transportation, Human Spaceflight, and Space Science, 1979-1988.* NASA SP-4012, 1999.

Rumerman, Judy A. *NASA Historical Data Book, Vol. VI: NASA Space Applications, Aeronautics and Space Research and Technology, Tracking and Data Acquisition/Support Operations, Commercial Programs, and Resources, 1979-1988.* NASA SP-4012, 1999.

Astronautics and Aeronautics Chronology

Eugene M. Emme, comp. *Aeronautics and Astronautics Chronology, 1915-1960. Aeronautics and Astronautics: An American Chronology of Science and Technology in the Exploration of Space, 1915-1960* (Washington, DC: National Aeronautics and Space Administration, 1961). Visit http://history.nasa.gov/series95.html for a pdf version of this document.

Eugene M. Emme, comp. *Aeronautical and Astronautical Events of 1961. Report of the National Aeronautics and Space Administration to the Committee on Science and Astronautics, U.S. House of Representatives, 87th Cong., 2d. Sess.* (Washington, DC: U.S. Government Printing Office, 1962). Visit http://history.nasa.gov/series95.html for a pdf version of this document.

Astronautical and Aeronautical Events of 1962. Report to the Committee on Science and Astronautics, Report to the Committee on Science and Astronautics, U.S. House of Representatives, Eighty-eighth Congress, first session (Washington, DC: U.S. Government Printing Office, 1963).

Astronautics and Aeronautics, 1963: Chronology of Science, Technology, and Policy. NASA SP-4004, 1964.

Astronautics and Aeronautics, 1964: Chronology of Science, Technology, and Policy. NASA SP-4005, 1965.

Astronautics and Aeronautics, 1965: Chronology of Science, Technology, and Policy. NASA SP-4006, 1966.

Astronautics and Aeronautics, 1966: Chronology of Science, Technology, and Policy. NASA SP-4007, 1967.

Astronautics and Aeronautics, 1967: Chronology of Science, Technology, and Policy. NASA SP-4008, 1968.

Astronautics and Aeronautics, 1968: Chronology of Science, Technology, and Policy. NASA SP-4010, 1969.

Astronautics and Aeronautics, 1969: Chronology of Science, Technology, and Policy. NASA SP-4014, 1970.

Astronautics and Aeronautics, 1970: Chronology of Science, Technology, and Policy. NASA SP-4015, 1972.

Astronautics and Aeronautics, 1971: Chronology of Science, Technology, and Policy. NASA SP-4016, 1972.

Astronautics and Aeronautics, 1972: Chronology of Science, Technology, and Policy. NASA SP-4017, 1974.

Astronautics and Aeronautics, 1973: Chronology of Science, Technology, and Policy. NASA SP-4018, 1975.

Astronautics and Aeronautics, 1974: Chronology of Science, Technology, and Policy. NASA SP-4019, 1977.

Astronautics and Aeronautics, 1975: Chronology of Science, Technology, and Policy. NASA SP-4020, 1979.

Astronautics and Aeronautics, 1976: Chronology of Science, Technology, and Policy. NASA SP-4021, 1984.

Astronautics and Aeronautics, 1977: Chronology of Science, Technology, and Policy. NASA SP-4022, 1986.

Astronautics and Aeronautics, 1978: Chronology of Science, Technology, and Policy. NASA SP-4023, 1986.

Astronautics and Aeronautics, 1979-1984: Chronology of Science, Technology, and Policy. NASA SP-4024, 1988.

Astronautics and Aeronautics, 1985: Chronology of Science, Technology, and Policy. NASA SP-4025, 1990.

Gawdiak, Ihor Y., Ramon J. Miro, and Sam Stueland, comps. *Astronautics and Aeronautics, 1986-1990: A Chronology*. NASA SP-4027, 1997.

Gawdiak, Ihor Y. and Shetland, Charles. *Astronautics and Aeronautics, 1991-1995: A Chronology*. NASA SP-2000-4028, 2000.

NASA Publications by Special Publication (SP) Numbers

Reference Works, NASA SP-4000

Grimwood, James M. *Project Mercury: A Chronology*. NASA SP-4001, 1963.

Grimwood, James M., and Barton C. Hacker, with Peter J. Vorzimmer. *Project Gemini Technology and Operations: A Chronology*. NASA SP-4002, 1969.

Link, Mae Mills. *Space Medicine in Project Mercury*. NASA SP-4003, 1965.

Ertel, Ivan D., and Mary Louise Morse. *The Apollo Spacecraft: A Chronology, Volume I, Through November 7, 1962*. NASA SP-4009, 1969.

Morse, Mary Louise, and Jean Kernahan Bays. *The Apollo Spacecraft: A Chronology, Volume II, November 8, 1962-September 30, 1964*. NASA SP-4009, 1973.

Brooks, Courtney G., and Ivan D. Ertel. *The Apollo Spacecraft: A Chronology, Volume III, October 1, 1964-January 20, 1966*. NASA SP-4009, 1973.

Ertel, Ivan D., and Roland W. Newkirk, with Courtney G. Brooks. *The Apollo Spacecraft: A Chronology, Volume IV, January 21, 1966-July 13, 1974*. NASA SP-4009, 1978.

Newkirk, Roland W., and Ivan D. Ertel, with Courtney G. Brooks. *Skylab: A Chronology*. NASA SP-4011, 1977.

Van Nimmen, Jane, and Leonard C. Bruno, with Robert L. Rosholt. *NASA Historical Data Book, Vol. I: NASA Resources, 1958-1968*. NASA SP-4012, 1976, rep. ed. 1988.

Ezell, Linda Neuman. *NASA Historical Data Book, Vol. II: Programs and Projects, 1958-1968*. NASA SP-4012, 1988.

Ezell, Linda Neuman. *NASA Historical Data Book, Vol. III: Programs and Projects, 1969-1978*. NASA SP-4012, 1988.

Gawdiak, Ihor, with Helen Fedor. *NASA Historical Data Book, Vol. IV: NASA Resources, 1969-1978*. NASA SP-4012, 1994.

Rumerman, Judy A. *NASA Historical Data Book, Vol. V: NASA Launch Systems, Space Transportation, Human Spaceflight, and Space Science, 1979-1988*. NASA SP-4012, 1999.

Rumerman, Judy A. *NASA Historical Data Book, Vol. VI: NASA Space Applications, Aeronautics and Space Research and Technology, Tracking and Data Acquisition/Support Operations, Commercial Programs, and Resources, 1979-1988*. NASA SP-4012, 1999.

Noordung, Hermann. *The Problem of Space Travel: The Rocket Motor*. Edited by Ernst Stuhlinger and J.D. Hunley, with Jennifer Garland. NASA SP-4026, 1995.

Gawdiak, Ihor Y., Ramon J. Miro, and Sam Stueland, comps. *Astronautics and Aeronautics, 1986-1990: A Chronology*. NASA SP-4027, 1997.

Gawdiak, Ihor Y. and Shetland, Charles. *Astronautics and Aeronautics, 1991-1995: A Chronology*. NASA SP-2000-4028, 2000.

Orloff, Richard W. *Apollo by the Numbers: A Statistical Reference*. NASA SP-2000-4029, 2000. Visit http://history.nasa.gov/series95.html for a pdf version of this document..

Management Histories, NASA SP-4100

Rosholt, Robert L. *An Administrative History of NASA, 1958-1963*. NASA SP-4101, 1966.

Levine, Arnold S. *Managing NASA in the Apollo Era*. NASA SP-4102, 1982.

Roland, Alex. *Model Research: The National Advisory Committee for Aeronautics, 1915-1958*. NASA SP-4103, 1985.

Fries, Sylvia D. NASA *Engineers and the Age of Apollo*. NASA SP-4104, 1992.

Glennan, T. Keith. *The Birth of NASA: The Diary of T. Keith Glennan*. Edited by J.D. Hunley. NASA SP-4105, 1993.

Seamans, Robert C. *Aiming at Targets: The Autobiography of Robert C. Seamans*. NASA SP-4106, 1996.

Garber, Stephen J., editor. *Looking Backward, Looking Forward: Forty Years of Human Spaceflight Symposium*. NASA SP-2002-4107.

Mallick, Donald L. with Peter W. Merlin. *The Smell of Kerosene: A Test Pilot's Odyssey*. NASA SP-4108.

Iliff, Kenneth W. and Curtis L. Peebles. *From Runway to Orbit: Reflections of a NASA Engineer*. NASA SP-2004-4109.

Laufer, Alexander, Post, Todd, and Hoffman, Edward. *Shared Voyage: Learning and Unlearning from Remarkable Projects*. NASA SP-2005-4111.

Dawson, Virginia P. and Bowles, Mark D. *Realizing the Dream of Flight: Biographical Essays in Honor of the Centennial of Flight, 1903-2003*. NASA SP-2005-4112.

Project Histories, NASA SP-4200:

Swenson, Loyd S., Jr., James M. Grimwood, and Charles C. Alexander. *This New Ocean: A History of Project Mercury*. NASA SP-4201, 1966, reprinted 1999.

Green, Constance McLaughlin, and Milton Lomask. *Vanguard: A History*. NASA SP-4202, 1970; rep. ed. Smithsonian Institution Press, 1971.

Hacker, Barton C., and James M. Grimwood. *On Shoulders of Titans: A History of Project Gemini*. NASA SP-4203, 1977, reprinted 2002.

Benson, Charles D. and William Barnaby Faherty. *Moonport: A History of Apollo Launch Facilities and Operations*. NASA SP-4204, 1978. University Press of Florida has republished the book in two volumes, *Gateway to the Moon* and *Moon Launch!*

Brooks, Courtney G., James M. Grimwood, and Loyd S. Swenson, Jr. *Chariots for Apollo: A History of Manned Lunar Spacecraft*. NASA SP- 4205, 1979.

Bilstein, Roger E. *Stages to Saturn: A Technological History of the Apollo/Saturn Launch Vehicles*. NASA SP-4206, 1980 and 1996. Reprinted by the University Press of Florida.

Compton, W. David, and Charles D. Benson. *Living and Working in Space: A History of Skylab*. NASA SP-4208, 1983.

Ezell, Edward Clinton, and Linda Neuman Ezell. *The Partnership: A History of the Apollo-Soyuz Test Project*. NASA SP-4209, 1978.

Hall, R. Cargill. *Lunar Impact: A History of Project Ranger*. NASA SP-4210, 1977.

Newell, Homer E. *Beyond the Atmosphere: Early Years of Space Science*. NASA SP-4211, 1980.

Ezell, Edward Clinton, and Linda Neuman Ezell. *On Mars: Exploration of the Red Planet, 1958-1978*. NASA SP-4212, 1984.

Pitts, John A. *The Human Factor: Biomedicine in the Manned Space Program to 1980*. NASA SP-4213, 1985.

Compton, W. David. *Where No Man Has Gone Before: A History of Apollo Lunar Exploration Missions*. NASA SP-4214, 1989.

Naugle, John E. *First Among Equals: The Selection of NASA Space Science Experiments*. NASA SP-4215, 1991.

Wallace, Lane E. *Airborne Trailblazer: Two Decades with NASA Langley's 737 Flying Laboratory*. NASA SP-4216, 1994.

Butrica, Andrew J. *Beyond the Ionosphere: Fifty Years of Satellite Communications*. NASA SP-4217, 1997.

Butrica, Andrew J. *To See the Unseen: A History of Planetary Radar Astronomy.* NASA SP-4218, 1996.

Mack, Pamela E., ed. *From Engineering Science to Big Science: The NACA and NASA Collier Trophy Research Project Winners.* NASA SP-4219, 1998.

Reed, R. Dale. *Wingless Flight: The Lifting Body Story.* NASA SP-4220, 1998.

Heppenheimer, T. A. *The Space Shuttle Decision: NASA's Search for a Reusable Space Vehicle.* NASA SP-4221, 1999.

Hunley, J. D., ed. *Toward Mach 2: The Douglas D-558 Program.* NASA SP-4222, 1999.

Swanson, Glen E., ed. *"Before This Decade is Out..." Personal Reflections on the Apollo Program.* NASA SP-4223, 1999.

Tomayko, James E. *Computers Take Flight: A History of NASA's Pioneering Digital Fly-By-Wire Project.* NASA SP-4224, 2000.

Morgan, Clay. *Shuttle-Mir: The United States and Russia Share History's Highest Stage.* NASA SP-2001-4225.

Leary, William M. *We Freeze to Please: A History of NASA's Icing Research Tunnel and the Quest for Safety.* NASA SP-2002-4226, 2002.

Mudgway, Douglas J. *Uplink-Downlink: A History of the Deep Space Network, 1957-1997.* NASA SP-2001-4227.

Dawson, Virginia P. and Mark D. Bowles. *Taming Liquid Hydrogen: The Centaur Upper Stage Rocket, 1958-2002.* NASA SP-2004-4230.

Meltzer, Michael. *Mission to Jupiter: A History of the Galileo Project.* NASA SP-2007-4231.

Heppenheimer, T.A. *Facing the Heat Barrier: A History of Hypersonics.* NASA SP-2007-4232. Visit http://history.nasa.gov/series 95.html for a pdf version of this document.

Tsiao, Sunny. *"Read You Loud and Clear!" The Story of NASA's Spaceflight Tracking and Data Network.* NASA SP-2007-4233.

Center Histories, NASA SP-4300:

Rosenthal, Alfred. *Venture into Space: Early Years of Goddard Space Flight Center.* NASA SP-4301, 1985.

Hartman, Edwin, P. *Adventures in Research: A History of Ames Research Center, 1940-1965.* NASA SP-4302, 1970.

Hallion, Richard P. *On the Frontier: Flight Research at Dryden, 1946-1981.* NASA SP-4303, 1984.

Muenger, Elizabeth A. *Searching the Horizon: A History of Ames Research Center, 1940-1976.* NASA SP-4304, 1985.

Hansen, James R. *Engineer in Charge: A History of the Langley Aeronautical Laboratory, 1917-1958.* NASA SP-4305, 1987.

Dawson, Virginia P. *Engines and Innovation: Lewis Laboratory and American Propulsion Technology.* NASA SP-4306, 1991.

Dethloff, Henry C. *"Suddenly Tomorrow Came...": A History of the Johnson Space Center, 1957-1990.* NASA SP-4307, 1993.

Hansen, James R. *Spaceflight Revolution: NASA Langley Research Center from Sputnik to Apollo.* NASA SP-4308, 1995.

Wallace, Lane E. *Flights of Discovery: An Illustrated History of the Dryden Flight Research Center.* NASA SP-4309, 1996.

Herring, Mack R. *Way Station to Space: A History of the John C. Stennis Space Center.* NASA SP-4310, 1997.

Wallace, Harold D., Jr. *Wallops Station and the Creation of an American Space Program.* NASA SP-4311, 1997.

Wallace, Lane E. *Dreams, Hopes, Realities. NASA's Goddard Space Flight Center: The First Forty Years.* NASA SP-4312, 1999.

Dunar, Andrew J. and Waring, Stephen P. *Power to Explore: A History of Marshall Space Flight Center, 1960-1990.* NASA SP-4313, 1999.

Bugos, Glenn E. *Atmosphere of Freedom: Sixty Years at the NASA Ames Research Center.* NASA SP-2000-4314, 2000.

Schultz, James. *Crafting Flight: Aircraft Pioneers and the Contributions of the Men and Women of NASA Langley Research Center.* NASA SP-2003-4316, 2003.

Bowles, Mark D. *Science in Flux: NASA's Nuclear Program at Plum Brook Station, 1955-2005.* NASA SP-2006-4317.

Wallace, Lane E. *Flights of Discovery: Sixty Years of Flight Research at the Dryden Flight Research Center.* NASA SP-4318, 2007.

General Histories, NASA SP-4400:

Corliss, William R. NASA *Sounding Rockets, 1958-1968: A Historical Summary.* NASA SP-4401, 1971.

Wells, Helen T., Susan H. Whiteley, and Carrie Karegeannes. *Origins of NASA Names.* NASA SP-4402, 1976.

Anderson, Frank W., Jr. Orders of Magnitude: A History of NACA and NASA, 1915-1980. NASA SP-4403, 1981.

Sloop, John L. *Liquid Hydrogen as a Propulsion Fuel, 1945-1959.* NASA SP-4404, 1978.

Roland, Alex. *A Spacefaring People: Perspectives on Early Spaceflight*. NASA SP-4405, 1985.

Bilstein, Roger E. *Orders of Magnitude: A History of the NACA and NASA, 1915-1990*. NASA SP-4406, 1989.

Siddiqi, Asif A., *Challenge to Apollo: The Soviet Union and the Space Race, 1945-1974*. NASA SP-2000-4408, 2000.

Hogan, Thor. *Mars Wars: The Rise and Fall of the Space Exploration Initiative*. NASA SP-2007-4410, 2007.

Monographs in Aerospace History (SP-4500 Series):

Launius, Roger D. and Aaron K. Gillette, comps. *Toward a History of the Space Shuttle: An Annotated Bibliography*. Monograph in Aerospace History, No. 1, 1992.

Launius, Roger D., and J.D. Hunley, comps. *An Annotated Bibliography of the Apollo Program*. Monograph in Aerospace History No. 2, 1994.

Launius, Roger D. *Apollo: A Retrospective Analysis*. Monograph in Aerospace History, No. 3, 1994.

Hansen, James R. *Enchanted Rendezvous: John C. Houbolt and the Genesis of the Lunar-Orbit Rendezvous Concept*. Monograph in Aerospace History, No. 4, 1995.

Gorn, Michael H. *Hugh L. Dryden's Career in Aviation and Space*. Monograph in Aerospace History, No. 5, 1996.

Powers, Sheryll Goecke. *Women in Flight Research at NASA Dryden Flight Research Center from 1946 to 1995*. Monograph in Aerospace History, No. 6, 1997.

Portree, David S.F. and Robert C. Trevino. *Walking to Olympus: An EVA Chronology*. Monograph in Aerospace History, No. 7, 1997.

Logsdon, John M., moderator. *Legislative Origins of the National Aeronautics and Space Act of 1958: Proceedings of an Oral History Workshop*. Monograph in Aerospace History, No. 8, 1998. Visit http://history.nasa.gov/series95.html for a pdf version of this document.

Rumerman, Judy A., comp. *U.S. Human Spaceflight, A Record of Achievement 1961-1998*. Monograph in Aerospace History, No. 9, 1998.

Portree, David S. F. *NASA's Origins and the Dawn of the Space Age*. Monograph in Aerospace History, No. 10, 1998.

Logsdon, John M. *Together in Orbit: The Origins of International Cooperation in the Space Station*. Monograph in Aerospace History, No. 11, 1998.

Phillips, W. Hewitt. *Journey in Aeronautical Research: A Career at NASA Langley Research Center*. Monograph in Aerospace History, No. 12, 1998.

Braslow, Albert L. *A History of Suction-Type Laminar-Flow Control with Emphasis on Flight Research.* Monograph in Aerospace History, No. 13, 1999.

Logsdon, John M., moderator. *Managing the Moon Program: Lessons Learned From Apollo.* Monograph in Aerospace History, No. 14, 1999.

Perminov, V.G. *The Difficult Road to Mars: A Brief History of Mars Exploration in the Soviet Union.* Monograph in Aerospace History, No. 15, 1999. Visit http://history.nasa.gov/series95.html for a pdf version of this document..

Tucker, Tom. *Touchdown: The Development of Propulsion Controlled Aircraft at NASA Dryden.* Monograph in Aerospace History, No. 16, 1999.

Maisel, Martin, Giulanetti, Demo J., and Dugan, Daniel C. *The History of the XV-15 Tilt Rotor Research Aircraft: From Concept to Flight.* Monograph in Aerospace History, No. 17, 2000.

Jenkins, Dennis R. *Hypersonics Before the Shuttle: A Concise History of the X-15 Research Airplane.* Monograph in Aerospace History, No. 18, 2000.

Chambers, Joseph R. *Partners in Freedom: Contributions of the Langley Research Center to U.S. Military Aircraft of the 1990s.* Monograph in Aerospace History, No. 19, 2000 (NASA SP-2000-4519).

Waltman, Gene L. *Black Magic and Gremlins: Analog Flight Simulations at NASA's Flight Research Center.* Monograph in Aerospace History, No. 20, 2000 (NASA SP-2000-4520).

Portree, David S.F. *Humans to Mars: Fifty Years of Mission Planning, 1950-2000.* Monograph in Aerospace History, No. 21, 2001 (NASA SP-2001-4521).

Thompson, Milton O. with J.D. Hunley. *Flight Research: Problems Encountered and What They Should Teach Us.* Monograph in Aerospace History, No. 22, 2001 (NASA SP-2001-4522).

Tucker, Tom. *The Eclipse Project.* Monograph in Aerospace History, No. 23, 2001 (NASA SP-2001-4523).

Siddiqi, Asif A. *Deep Space Chronicle: A Chronology of Deep Space and Planetary Probes 1958-2000.* Monograph in Aerospace History, No. 24, 2002 (NASA SP-2002-4524).

Merlin, Peter W. *Mach 3+: NASA/USAF YF-12 Flight Research, 1969-1979.* Monograph in Aerospace History, No. 25, 2001 (NASA SP-2001-4525).

Anderson, Seth B. *Memoirs of an Aeronautical Engineer: Flight Tests at Ames Research Center: 1940-1970.* Monograph in Aerospace History, No. 26, 2002 (NASA SP-2002-4526)

Renstrom, Arthur G. *Wilbur and Orville Wright: A Bibliography Commemorating the One-Hundredth Anniversary of the First Powered Flight on December 17, 1903.* Monograph in Aerospace History, No. 27, 2002 (NASA SP-2002-4527).

No monograph 28.

Chambers, Joseph R. *Concept to Reality: Contributions of the NASA Langley Research Center to U.S. Civil Aircraft of the 1990s*. Monograph in Aerospace History, No. 29, 2003. (SP-2003-4529).

Peebles, Curtis, editor. *The Spoken Word: Recollections of Dryden History, The Early Years*. Monograph in Aerospace History, No. 30, 2003. (SP-2003-4530).

Jenkins, Dennis R., Tony Landis, and Jay Miller. *American X-Vehicles: An Inventory- X-1 to X-50*. Monograph in Aerospace History, No. 31, 2003 (SP-2003-4531).

Renstrom, Arthur G. *Wilbur and Orville Wright: A Chronology Commemorating the One-Hundredth Anniversary of the First Powered Flight on December 17, 1903*. Monograph in Aerospace History, No. 32, 2003. (NASA SP-2003-4532).

Bowles, Mark D. and Arrighi, Robert S. *NASA's Nuclear Frontier: The Plum Brook Research Reactor*. Monograph in Aerospace History, No. 33, 2004. (SP-2004-4533).

Matranga, Gene J.; Wayne C. Ottinger; Calvin R.; Jarvis, and D. Christian Gelzer. *Unconventional, Contrary, and Ugly: The Lunar Landing Research Vehicle*. Monograph in Aerospace History, No. 35, 2006. (NASA SP-2004-4535).

McCurdy, Howard E. *Low Cost Innovation in Spaceflight: The History of the Near Earth Asteroid Rendezvous (NEAR) Mission*. Monograph in Aerospace History, No. 36, 2005. (NASA SP-2005-4536).

Seamans, Robert C. Jr. *Project Apollo: The Tough Decisions*. Monograph in Aerospace History, No. 37, 2005. (NASA SP-2005-4537).

Lambright, W. Henry. *NASA and the Environment: The Case of Ozone Depletion*. Monograph in Aerospace History, No. 38, 2005. (NASA SP-2005-4538).

Chambers, Joseph R. *Innovation in Flight: Research of the NASA Langley Research Center on Revolutionary Advanced Concepts for Aeronautics*. Monograph in Aerospace History, No. 39, 2005. (NASA SP-2005-4539). This monograph is only available on-line. Visit http://history.nasa.gov/series95.html.

Phillips, W. Hewitt. *Journey Into Space Research: Continuation of a Career at NASA Langley Research Center*. Monograph in Aerospace History, No. 40, 2005. (NASA SP-2005-4540). This monograph is only available on-line. Visit http://history.nasa.gov/series95.html.

Rumerman, Judy A., comp. *U.S. Human Spaceflight: A Record of Achievement, 1961-2006*. Monograph in Aerospace History No. 41, 2007. (NASA SP-2007-4541). This is an updating by Chris Gamble and Gabriel Okolski of the similarly titled Monograph 9 that was published in 1998.

Dryden Historical Studies

Tomayko, James E., and Christian Gelzer, editor. *The Story of Self-Repairing Flight Control Systems*. Dryden Historical Study #1.

Dana, William H. *X-38: Flight Testing the Prototype Crew Recovery Vehicle*. Dryden Historical Study #2.

Electronic Media (SP-4600 Series)

Remembering Apollo 11: The 30th Anniversary Data Archive CD-ROM. (NASA SP-4601, 1999)

Remembering Apollo 11: The 35th Anniversary Data Archive CD-ROM. (NASA SP-2004-4601, 2004). This is an update of the 1999 edition.

The Mission Transcript Collection: U.S. Human Spaceflight Missions from Mercury Redstone 3 to Apollo 17. (SP-2000-4602, 2001). Available commercially from CG Publishing.

Shuttle-Mir: the United States and Russia Share History's Highest Stage. (NASA SP-2001-4603, 2002). This CD-ROM is available from NASA CORE.

U.S. Centennial of Flight Commission presents Born of Dreams ~ Inspired by Freedom. (NASA SP-2004-4604, 2004).

Of Ashes and Atoms: A Documentary on the NASA Plum Brook Reactor Facility. (NASA SP-2005-4605).

Taming Liquid Hydrogen: The Centaur Upper Stage Rocket Interactive CD-ROM. (NASA SP-2004-4606, 2004).

Fueling Space Exploration: The History of NASA's Rocket Engine Test Facility DVD. (NASA SP-2005-4607).

Altitude Wind Tunnel at NASA Glenn Research Center. An Interactive History. (NASA SP-2008-4608).

Conference Proceedings (SP-4700 Series)

Dick, Steven J. and Cowing, Keith L, ed. R*isk and Exploration: Earth, Sea and the Stars.* (NASA SP-2005-4701).

Dick, Steven J. and Launius, Roger D. *Critical Issues in the History of Spaceflight.* (NASA SP-2006-4702).

Historical Reports (NASA HHR)

Boone, W. Fred. *NASA Office of Defense Affairs: The First Five Years.* (NASA HHR-32, 1970).

Research in NASA History: A Guide to the NASA History Program. (NASA HHR-64, revised June 1997).

NASA Special Reports (NASA SP-4900)

Kloman, Erasmus H. *Unmanned Space Project Management: Surveyor and Lunar Orbiter.* (NASA SP-4901, 1972).

Other NASA Special Publications, not in the formal NASA History Series

The Impact of Science on Society. NASA SP-482 by James Burke, Jules Bergman, and Isaac Asimov, 1985.

Space Station Requirements and Transportation Options for Lunar Outpost. NASA, 1990.

Space Station Freedom Accommodation of the Human Exploration Initiative. NASA, 1990.

Why Man Explores. NASA EP-125, 1976.

Results of the Second Manned Suborbital Space Flight, July 21, 1961. NASA, 1961.

Results of the Second U.S. Manned Orbital Space Flight. NASA SP-6, 1962.

Results of the Third U.S. Manned Orbital Space Flight. NASA SP-12, 1962.

Mercury Project Summary including Results of the Fourth Manned Orbital Flight. NASA SP-45, 1963.

X-15 Research Results With a Selected Bibliography. NASA SP-60, 1965.

Exploring Space with a Camera. NASA SP-168, 1968.

Aerospace Food Technology. NASA SP-202, 1969.

What Made Apollo a Success? NASA SP-287, 1971.

Evolution of the Solar System. NASA SP-345, 1976.

Pioneer Odyssey (NASA SP-349/396, revised edition, 1977) by Richard Fimmel, William Swindell, and Eric Burgess.

Apollo Expeditions to the Moon. NASA SP-350, 1975.

Apollo Over the Moon: A View From Orbit. (NASA SP-362, 1978) edited by Harold Masursky, G.W. Colton, and Farouk El-Baz.

Introduction to the Aerodynamics of Flight. (NASA SP-367, 1975) by Theodore A. Talay.

Biomedical Results of Apollo. (NASA SP-368, 1975), edited by Richard S. Johnston, Lawrence F. Dietlein, M.D., and Charles A. Berry, M.D.

Skylab EREP Investigations Summary. (NASA SP-399, 1978)

Skylab: Our First Space Station. (NASA SP-400, 1977), edited by Leland F. Belew.

Skylab, Classroom in Space. (NASA SP-401, 1977), edited by Lee Summerlin.

A New Sun: Solar Results from Skylab. (NASA SP-402, 1979) by John A. Eddy and edited by Rein Ise.

Skylab's Astronomy and Space Sciences. (NASA SP-404, 1979), edited by Charles A. Lundquist.

The Space Shuttle. (NASA SP-407, 1976)

The Search For Extraterrestrial Intelligence. (NASA SP-419, 1977), edited by Philip Morrison, John Billingham, and John Wolfe.

Atlas of Mercury. (NASA SP-423, 1978) by Merton E. Davies, Stephen E. Dwornik, et. al.

The Voyage of Mariner 10: Mission to Venus and Mercury. (NASA SP-424, 1978) by James A. Dunne and Eric Burgess.

The Martian Landscape. (NASA SP-425, 1978)

The Space Shuttle at Work. (NASA SP-432/EP-156 1979) by Howard Allaway.

Project Orion: A Design Study of a System for Detecting Extrasolar Planets. (NASA SP-436, 1980), edited by David C. Black.

Wind Tunnels of NASA. (NASA SP-440, 1981).

Viking Orbiter Views of Mars. (NASA SP-441, 1980)

The High Speed Frontier: Case Histories of Four NACA Programs, 1920-1950. (NASA SP-445, 1980.)

The Star Splitters: The High Energy Astronomy Observatories. (NASA SP-466, 1984) by Wallace H. Tucker.

Planetary Geology in the 1980s. (NASA SP-467, 1985) by Joseph Veverka.

Quest for Performance: The Evolution of Modern Aircraft. (NASA SP-468, 1985.)

The Long Duration Exposure Facility (LDEF): Mission 1 Experiments. (SP-473, 1984) ed. by Lenwood G. Clark, William H. Kinar, et. al.

Voyager 1 and 2, Atlas of Saturnian Satellites. (NASA SP-474, 1984) edited by Raymond Batson.

Far Travelers: The Exploring Machines. (NASA SP-480, 1985) by Oran W. Nicks.

Living Aloft: Human Requirements for Extended Spaceflight. (NASA SP-483, 1985)

Space Shuttle Avionics System. (NASA SP-504, 1989) by John F. Hanaway and Robert W. Moorehead.

Life Into Space: Space Life Sciences Research, Volumes I - III. 1965-2003 (NASA SP-534).

Flight Research at Ames, 1940-1997. (NASA SP-3300, 1998).

The Planetary Quarantine Program. (NASA SP-4902, 1974).

Spaceborne Digital Computer Systems. (NASA SP-8070, 1971).

Magellan: The Unveiling of Venus. (JPL-400-345, 1989)

Guide to Magellan Image Interpretation. (JPL-93-24) by John Ford, Jeffrey Plaut, et. al.

The Apollo Program Summary Report. (Document # JSC-09423, April 1975)

Saturn Illustrated Chronology. (MHR-5, Marshall Space Flight Center, fifth edition, 1971) prepared by David S. Akens.

Celebrating a Century of Flight. (NASA SP-2002-09-511-HQ). Edited by Tony Springer.

Present and Future State of the Art in Guidance Computer Memories. (NASA TN D-4224, 1967) by Robert C. Ricci.

NASA Educational Publications

Apollo 13 "Houston, we've got a problem." (NASA EP-76, 1970).

On the Moon with Apollo 16: A Guide to the Descartes Region. (NASA EP-95, 1972)

Skylab: A Guidebook. (NASA EP-107, 1973), by Leland F. Belew and Ernst Stuhlinger.

Spacelab: An International Short-Stay Orbiting Laboratory. (NASA EP-165) by Walter Froehlich.

A Meeting with the Universe: Science Discoveries from the Space Program. (NASA EP-177, 1981).

NASA Publications (NPs)

Science in Orbit: The Shuttle & Spacelab Experience: 1981-1986. (NASA NP-119, 1988).

NASA Conference Proceedings

Life in the Universe: Proceedings of a conference held at NASA Ames Research Center Moffet Field, California, June 19-20, 1979. (NASA CP-2156, 1981), edited by John Billingham.

Proceedings of the X-15 First Flight 30th Anniversary Celebration of June 8, 1989.

NASA Technical Memoranda

Destination Moon: A History of the Lunar Orbiter Program. (NASA TM-3487, 1977) by Bruce Byers.

New Series in NASA History Published by the American Institute of Aeronautics and Astronautics.

Peebles, Curtis. *The X-43A Flight Research Program: Lessons Learned on the Road to Mach 10.* AIAA, 2008.

Merlin, Peter. *From Archangel to Senior Crown: The Design and Development of the Blackbird.* AIAA, 2008.

New Series in NASA History Published by the Johns Hopkins University Press:

Cooper, Henry S. F., Jr. *Before Lift-off: The Making of a Space Shuttle Crew*. Baltimore: Johns Hopkins University Press, 1987.

McCurdy, Howard E. *The Space Station Decision: Incremental Politics and Technological Choice*. Baltimore: Johns Hopkins University Press, 1990.

Hufbauer, Karl. *Exploring the Sun: Solar Science Since Galileo*. Baltimore: Johns Hopkins University Press, 1991.

McCurdy, Howard E. *Inside NASA: High Technology and Organizational Change in the U.S. Space Program*. Baltimore: Johns Hopkins University Press, 1993.

Lambright, W. Henry. *Powering Apollo: James E. Webb of NASA*. Baltimore: Johns Hopkins University Press, 1995.

Bromberg, Joan Lisa. *NASA and the Space Industry*. Baltimore: Johns Hopkins University Press, 1999.

Beattie, Donald A. *Taking Science to the Moon: Lunar Experiments and the Apollo Program*. Baltimore: Johns Hopkins University Press, 2001.

McCurdy, Howard E. Faster, *Better, Cheaper: Low-Cost Innovation in the U.S. Space Program*. Baltimore: Johns Hopkins University Press, 2001.

Johnson, Stephen B. *The Secret of Apollo: Systems Management in American and European Space Programs*. Baltimore: Johns Hopkins University Press, 2002.

Lambright, W. Henry, editor. *Space Policy in the 21st Century*. Baltimore: Johns Hopkins University Press, 2002.

Bilstein, Roger E. *Testing Aircraft, Exploring Space: An Illustrated History of NACA and NASA*. Baltimore: Johns Hopkins University Press, 2003.

Butrica, Andrew J. *Single Stage to Orbit: Politics, Space Technology, and the Quest for Reusable Rocketry*. Baltimore: Johns Hopkins University Press, 2005.

Conway, Erik M. *High-Speed Dreams: NASA and the Technopolitics of Supersonic Transportation, 1945-1999*. Baltimore: Johns Hopkins University Press, 2005.

Launius, Roger D. and Howard E. McCurdy. *Robots in Space: Technology, Evolution, and Interplanetary Travel*. Baltimore: Johns Hopkins University Press, 2008.

Conway, Erik M. *Atmospheric Science at NASA: A History*. Baltimore: Johns Hopkins University Press, 2008.

NASA History Titles Published by Texas A&M University Press

Schorn, Ronald A. *Planetary Astronomy: From Ancient Times to the Third Millennium*. College Station: Texas A&M University Press, 1998.

NASA History Titles Published by The University Press of Kentucky

Gorn, Michael H. *Expanding the Envelope: Flight Research at NACA and NASA*. Lexington: The University Press of Kentucky, 2001.

Reed, R. Dale. *Wingless Flight: The Lifting Body Story*. Lexington: The University Press of Kentucky, 2002.

Ed. by Launius, Roger D. and Dennis R. Jenkins. *To Reach the High Frontier: A History of U.S. Launch Vehicles*. Lexington: The University Press of Kentucky, 2002.

NASA History Titles Published by the University Press of Florida

Ed. by Swanson, Glen W. *"Before This Decade is Out..." : Personal Reflections on the Apollo Program*. Gainesville: The University Press of Florida, 2002.

Benson, Charles D. and William B. Faherty. *Moon Launch!: A History of the Saturn-Apollo Launch Operations*. Gainesville: The University Press of Florida, 2001.

Benson, Charles D. and William B. Faherty. *Gateway to the Moon: Building the Kennedy Space Center Launch Complex*. Gainesville: The University Press of Florida, 2001.

Bilstein, Roger E. *Stages to Saturn: A Technological History of the Apollo/Saturn Launch Vehicles*. (Originally published as NASA SP-4206 in 1980 and reprinted in 1996). Gainesville: The University Press of Florida, 2003.

Siddiqi, Asif A. *The Soviet Space Race with Apollo*. Gainesville: The University Press of Florida, 2003.

Siddiqi, Asif A. *Sputnik and the Soviet Space Challenge*. Gainesville: The University Press of Florida, 2003.

Lipartito, Kenneth and Butler, Orville R. *A History of the Kennedy Space Center*. Gainesville: The University Press of Florida, 2007.

NASA History Titles Published by Harwood Academic Press

Ed. by Roger D. Launius, John M. Logsdon and Robert W. Smith. *Reconsidering Sputnik: Forty Years Since the Soviet Satellite*. London: Harwood Academic Press, 2000.

NASA History Titles Published by the University of Illinois Press

Ed. by Roger D. Launius and Howard McCurdy. *Spaceflight and the Myth of Presidential Leadership*. Urbana, IL: University of Illinois Press, 1997.

NASA History Titles Published by Greenwood Press

Launius, Roger D. *Frontiers of Space Exploration*. Westport, CT: Greenwood Press, 1998.

NASA History Titles Published by the Smithsonian Institution Press

Heppenheimer, T.A. *Development of the Shuttle, 1972-1981*. Washington, DC: Smithsonian Institution Press, 2002.

Dethloff, Henry C. and Ronald A. Schorn. *Voyager's Grand Tour: To the Outer Planets and Beyond*. Washington, DC: Smithsonian Institution Press, 2003.

Hallion, Richard P. and Michael H. Gorn. *On the Frontier: Experimental Flight at NASA Dryden*. Washington, DC: Smithsonian Institution Press, 2003.

NASA History Titles Published by CG Publishing, Inc.

The Mission Transcript Collection: U.S. Human Spaceflight Missions From Mercury Redstone 3 to Apollo 17. (NASA SP-2000-4602).

NASA History Titles Published by Abrams Press

Dick, Steven, editor, et. al. *America In Space: NASA's First Fifty Years*. New York: Abrams, 2007.

America in Space, published by Harry N. Abrams, Inc., New York.

Miscellaneous Publications of NASA History

Dawson, Virginia. *Ideas Into Hardware: A History of the Rocket Engine Test Facility at the NASA Glenn Research Center*. Cleveland, 2004.

9781780393100